GO!

with

Windows Vista™

Getting Started

Shelley Gaskin and Robert L. Ferrett

PEARSON

Prentice
Hall

Upper Saddle River, New Jersey

This book is dedicated to my students, who inspire me every day, and to my husband, Fred Gaskin.
—Shelley Gaskin

We dedicate this book to our granddaughters, who bring us great joy and happiness:
Clara and Siena & Alexis and Grace.
—Robert L. Ferrett

Library of Congress Cataloging-in-Publication Data

Gaskin, Shelley.
  Go! with Windows Vista: getting started / Shelley Gaskin and Robert L. Ferrett.
      p. cm.
  Includes index.
  ISBN 0-13-614097-1
  1. Microsoft Windows (Computer file) 2. Operating systems (Computers). I. Ferrett, Robert. II. Title.
  QA76.76.O63G392 2007
  005.4'46--dc22

                                                    2007011773

Vice President and Publisher: Natalie E. Anderson
Associate VP/Executive Acquisitions Editor,
  Print: Stephanie Wall
Executive Acquisitions Editor, Media: Richard Keaveny
Product Development Manager: Eileen Bien Calabro
Editorial Project Manager: Laura Burgess
Development Editor: Ginny Munroe
Editorial Assistants: Becky Knauer, Lora Cimiluca
Content Development Manager: Cathi Profitko
Production Media Project Manager: Lorena Cerisano
Senior Media Project Manager: Steve Gagliostro
Director of Marketing: Margaret Waples
Senior Marketing Manager: Jason Sakos
Marketing Assistants: Angela Frey, Kathryn Ferranti
Sales Associate: Rebecca Scott

Managing Editor: Lynda J. Castillo
Production Project Manager: Wanda Rockwell
Production Editor: GGS Book Services
Photo Researcher: GGS Book Services
Manufacturing Buyer: Natacha Moore
Production/Editorial Assistant: Sandra K. Bernales
Design Director: Maria Lange
Art Director/Interior Design: Blair Brown
Cover Photo: Courtesy of Getty Images, Inc./Marvin
  Mattelson
Composition: GGS Book Services
Project Management: GGS Book Services
Cover Printer: Phoenix Color
Printer/Binder: RR Donnelley/Willard

Microsoft, Windows Vista, Word, Excel, Access, PowerPoint, Outlook, FrontPage, Visual Basic, MSN, The Microsoft Network, and/or other Microsoft products referenced herein are either trademarks or registered trademarks of Microsoft Corporation in the U.S.A. and other countries. Screen shots and icons reprinted with permission from the Microsoft Corporation. This book is not sponsored or endorsed by or affiliated with Microsoft Corporation.

Credits and acknowledgments borrowed from other sources and reproduced, with permission, in this textbook are as follows or on the appropriate page within the text.

10 9 8 7 6 5 4 3 2
ISBN-10: 0-13-614097-1
ISBN-13: 978-0-13-614097-1

Table of Contents

Letter from the Editor

Dear Instructors and Students,

The primary goal of the *GO!* Series is two-fold. The first goal is to help instructors teach the course they want in less time. The second goal is to provide students with the skills to solve business problems using the computer as a tool, for both themselves and the organization for which they might be employed.

The *GO!* Series was originally created by Series Editor Shelley Gaskin and published with the release of Microsoft Office 2003. Her ideas came from years of using textbooks that didn't meet all the needs of today's diverse classroom and that were too confusing for students. Shelley continues to enhance the series by ensuring we stay true to our vision of developing quality instruction and useful classroom tools.

But we also need your input and ideas.

Over time, the *GO!* Series has evolved based on direct feedback from instructors and students using the series. *We are the publisher that listens.* To publish a textbook that works for you, it's critical that we continue to listen to this feedback. It's important to me to talk with you and hear your stories about using *GO!* Your voice can make a difference.

My hope is that this letter will inspire you to write me an e-mail and share your thoughts on using the *GO!* Series.

Stephanie Wall
Executive Editor, *GO!* Series
stephanie_wall@prenhall.com

GO! System Contributors

We thank the following people for their hard work and support in making the *GO!* System all that it is!

Additional Author Support

Coyle, Diane	Montgomery County Community College
Fry, Susan	Boise State
Townsend, Kris	Spokane Falls Community College
Stroup, Tracey	Amgen Corporation

Instructor Resource Authors

Amer, Beverly	Northern Arizona University	Paterson, Jim	Paradise Valley Community College
Boito, Nancy	Harrisburg Area Community College	Prince, Lisa	Missouri State
Coyle, Diane	Montgomery County Community College	Rodgers, Gwen	Southern Nazarene University
Dawson, Tamara	Southern Nazarene University	Ruymann, Amy	Burlington Community College
Driskel, Loretta	Niagara County Community College	Ryan, Bob	Montgomery County Community College
Elliott, Melissa	Odessa College		
Fry, Susan	Boise State	Smith, Diane	Henry Ford College
Geoghan, Debra	Bucks County Community College	Spangler, Candice	Columbus State Community College
Hearn, Barbara	Community College of Philadelphia	Thompson, Joyce	Lehigh Carbon Community College
Jones, Stephanie	South Plains College	Tiffany, Janine	Reading Area Community College
Madsen, Donna	Kirkwood Community College	Watt, Adrienne	Douglas College
Meck, Kari	Harrisburg Area Community College	Weaver, Paul	Bossier Parish Community College
Miller, Cindy	Ivy Tech	Weber, Sandy	Gateway Technical College
Nowakowski, Tony	Buffalo State	Wood, Dawn	
Pace, Phyllis	Queensborough Community College	Weissman, Jonathan	Finger Lakes Community College

Super Reviewers

Brotherton, Cathy	Riverside Community College	Maurer, Trina	Odessa College
Cates, Wally	Central New Mexico Community College	Meck, Kari	Harrisburg Area Community College
		Miller, Cindy	Ivy Tech Community College
Cone, Bill	Northern Arizona University	Nielson, Phil	Salt Lake Community College
Coverdale, John	Riverside Community College	Rodgers, Gwen	Southern Nazarene University
Foster, Nancy	Baker College	Smolenski, Robert	Delaware Community College
Helfand, Terri	Chaffey College	Spangler, Candice	Columbus State Community College
Hibbert, Marilyn	Salt Lake Community College	Thompson, Joyce	Lehigh Carbon Community College
Holliday, Mardi	Community College of Philadelphia	Weber, Sandy	Gateway Technical College
Jerry, Gina	Santa Monica College	Wells, Lorna	Salt Lake Community College
Martin, Carol	Harrisburg Area Community College	Zaboski, Maureen	University of Scranton

Technical Editors

Janice Snyder
Joyce Nielsen
Colette Eisele
Janet Pickard
Mara Zebest
Lindsey Allen
William Daley

Student Reviewers

Allen, John	Asheville-Buncombe Tech Community College	Erickson, Mike	Ball State University
		Gadomski, Amanda	Northern Michigan University
Alexander, Steven	St. Johns River Community College	Gyselinck, Craig	Central Washington University
Alexander, Melissa	Tulsa Community College	Harrison, Margo	Central Washington University
Bolz, Stephanie	Northern Michigan University	Heacox, Kate	Central Washington University
Berner, Ashley	Central Washington University	Hill, Cheretta	Northwestern State University
Boomer, Michelle	Northern Michigan University	Innis, Tim	Tulsa Community College
Busse, Brennan	Northern Michigan University	Jarboe, Aaron	Central Washington University
Butkey, Maura	Central Washington University	Klein, Colleen	Northern Michigan University
Christensen, Kaylie	Northern Michigan University	Moeller, Jeffrey	Northern Michigan University
Connally, Brianna	Central Washington University	Nicholson, Regina	Athens Tech College
Davis, Brandon	Northern Michigan University	Niehaus, Kristina	Northern Michigan University
Davis, Christen	Central Washington University	Nisa, Zaibun	Santa Rosa Community College
Den Boer, Lance	Central Washington University	Nunez, Nohelia	Santa Rosa Community College
Dix, Jessica	Central Washington University	Oak, Samantha	Central Washington University
Moeller, Jeffrey	Northern Michigan University	Oertii, Monica	Central Washington University
Downs, Elizabeth	Central Washington University	Palenshus, Juliet	Central Washington University

Pohl, Amanda	Northern Michigan University	Shanahan, Megan	Northern Michigan University
Presnell, Randy	Central Washington University	Teska, Erika	Hawaii Pacific University
Ritner, April	Northern Michigan University	Traub, Amy	Northern Michigan University
Rodriguez, Flavia	Northwestern State University	Underwood, Katie	Central Washington University
Roberts, Corey	Tulsa Community College	Walters, Kim	Central Washington University
Rossi, Jessica Ann	Central Washington University	Wilson, Kelsie	Central Washington University
Shafapay, Natasha	Central Washington University	Wilson, Amanda	Green River Community College

Series Reviewers

Abraham, Reni	Houston Community College	Crawford, Thomasina	Miami-Dade College, Kendall Campus
Agatston, Ann	Agatston Consulting Technical College	Credico, Grace	Lethbridge Community College
Alexander, Melody	Ball Sate University	Crenshaw, Richard	Miami Dade Community College, North
Alejandro, Manuel	Southwest Texas Junior College	Crespo, Beverly	Mt. San Antonio College
Ali, Farha	Lander University	Crossley, Connie	Cincinnati State Technical Community College
Amici, Penny	Harrisburg Area Community College		
Anderson, Patty A.	Lake City Community College	Curik, Mary	Central New Mexico Community College
Andrews, Wilma	Virginia Commonwealth College, Nebraska University	De Arazoza, Ralph	Miami Dade Community College
Anik, Mazhar	Tiffin University	Danno, John	DeVry University/Keller Graduate School
Armstrong, Gary	Shippensburg University		
Atkins, Bonnie	Delaware Technical Community College	Davis, Phillip	Del Mar College
		DeHerrera, Laurie	Pikes Peak Community College
Bachand, LaDonna	Santa Rosa Community College	Delk, Dr. K. Kay	Seminole Community College
Bagui, Sikha	University of West Florida	Doroshow, Mike	Eastfield College
Beecroft, Anita	Kwantlen University College	Douglas, Gretchen	SUNYCortland
Bell, Paula	Lock Haven College	Dove, Carol	Community College of Allegheny
Belton, Linda	Springfield Tech. Community College	Driskel, Loretta	Niagara Community College
		Duckwiler, Carol	Wabaunsee Community College
Bennett, Judith	Sam Houston State University	Duncan, Mimi	University of Missouri-St. Louis
Bhatia, Sai	Riverside Community College	Duthie, Judy	Green River Community College
Bishop, Frances	DeVry Institute—Alpharetta (ATL)	Duvall, Annette	Central New Mexico Community College
Blaszkiewicz, Holly	Ivy Tech Community College/Region 1		
Branigan, Dave	DeVry University	Ecklund, Paula	Duke University
Bray, Patricia	Allegany College of Maryland	Eng, Bernice	Brookdale Community College
Brotherton, Cathy	Riverside Community College	Evans, Billie	Vance-Granville Community College
Buehler, Lesley	Ohlone College	Feuerbach, Lisa	Ivy Tech East Chicago
Buell, C	Central Oregon Community College	Fisher, Fred	Florida State University
Byars, Pat	Brookhaven College	Foster, Penny L.	Anne Arundel Community College
Byrd, Lynn	Delta State University, Cleveland, Mississippi	Foszcz, Russ	McHenry County College
		Fry, Susan	Boise State University
Cacace, Richard N.	Pensacola Junior College	Fustos, Janos	Metro State
Cadenhead, Charles	Brookhaven College	Gallup, Jeanette	Blinn College
Calhoun, Ric	Gordon College	Gelb, Janet	Grossmont College
Cameron, Eric	Passaic Community College	Gentry, Barb	Parkland College
Carriker, Sandra	North Shore Community College	Gerace, Karin	St. Angela Merici School
Cannamore, Madie	Kennedy King	Gerace, Tom	Tulane University
Carreon, Cleda	Indiana University—Purdue University, Indianapolis	Ghajar, Homa	Oklahoma State University
		Gifford, Steve	Northwest Iowa Community College
Chaffin, Catherine	Shawnee State University	Glazer, Ellen	Broward Community College
Chauvin, Marg	Palm Beach Community College, Boca Raton	Gordon, Robert	Hofstra University
		Gramlich, Steven	Pasco-Hernando Community College
Challa, Chandrashekar	Virginia State University	Graviett, Nancy M.	St. Charles Community College, St. Peters, Missouri
Chamlou, Afsaneh	NOVA Alexandria		
Chapman, Pam	Wabaunsee Community College	Greene, Rich	Community College of Allegheny County
Christensen, Dan	Iowa Western Community College		
Clay, Betty	Southeastern Oklahoma State University	Gregoryk, Kerry	Virginia Commonwealth State
		Griggs, Debra	Bellevue Community College
Collins, Linda D.	Mesa Community College	Grimm, Carol	Palm Beach Community College
Conroy-Link, Janet	Holy Family College	Hahn, Norm	Thomas Nelson Community College
Cosgrove, Janet	Northwestern CT Community	Hammerschlag, Dr. Bill	Brookhaven College
Courtney, Kevin	Hillsborough Community College	Hansen, Michelle	Davenport University
Cox, Rollie	Madison Area Technical College	Hayden, Nancy	Indiana University—Purdue University, Indianapolis
Crawford, Hiram	Olive Harvey College		

Contributors continued

Hayes, Theresa	Broward Community College	Lord, Alexandria	Asheville Buncombe Tech
Helfand, Terri	Chaffey College	Lowe, Rita	Harold Washington College
Helms, Liz	Columbus State Community College	Low, Willy Hui	Joliet Junior College
Hernandez, Leticia	TCI College of Technology	Lucas, Vickie	Broward Community College
Hibbert, Marilyn	Salt Lake Community College	Lynam, Linda	Central Missouri State University
Hoffman, Joan	Milwaukee Area Technical College	Lyon, Lynne	Durham College
Hogan, Pat	Cape Fear Community College	Lyon, Pat Rajski	Tomball College
Holland, Susan	Southeast Community College	MacKinnon, Ruth	Georgia Southern University
Hopson, Bonnie	Athens Technical College	Macon, Lisa	Valencia Community College, West Campus
Horvath, Carrie	Albertus Magnus College		
Horwitz, Steve	Community College of Philadelphia	Machuca, Wayne	College of the Sequoias
Hotta, Barbara	Leeward Community College	Madison, Dana	Clarion University
Howard, Bunny	St. Johns River Community	Maguire, Trish	Eastern New Mexico University
Howard, Chris	DeVry University	Malkan, Rajiv	Montgomery College
Huckabay, Jamie	Austin Community College	Manning, David	Northern Kentucky University
Hudgins, Susan	East Central University	Marcus, Jacquie	Niagara Community College
Hulett, Michelle J.	Missouri State University	Marghitu, Daniela	Auburn University
Hunt, Darla A.	Morehead State University, Morehead, Kentucky	Marks, Suzanne	Bellevue Community College
		Marquez, Juanita	El Centro College
Hunt, Laura	Tulsa Community College	Marquez, Juan	Mesa Community College
Jacob, Sherry	Jefferson Community College	Martyn, Margie	Baldwin-Wallace College
Jacobs, Duane	Salt Lake Community College	Marucco, Toni	Lincoln Land Community College
Jauken, Barb	Southeastern Community	Mason, Lynn	Lubbock Christian University
Johnson, Kathy	Wright College	Matutis, Audrone	Houston Community College
Johnson, Mary	Kingwood College	Matkin, Marie	University of Lethbridge
Johnson, Mary	Mt. San Antonio College	McCain, Evelynn	Boise State University
Jones, Stacey	Benedict College	McCannon, Melinda	Gordon College
Jones, Warren	University of Alabama, Birmingham	McCarthy, Marguerite	Northwestern Business College
Jordan, Cheryl	San Juan College	McCaskill, Matt L.	Brevard Community College
Kapoor, Bhushan	California State University, Fullerton	McClellan, Carolyn	Tidewater Community College
Kasai, Susumu	Salt Lake Community College	McClure, Darlean	College of Sequoias
Kates, Hazel	Miami Dade Community College, Kendall	McCrory, Sue A.	Missouri State University
		McCue, Stacy	Harrisburg Area Community College
Keen, Debby	University of Kentucky	McEntire-Orbach, Teresa	Middlesex County College
Keeter, Sandy	Seminole Community College	McLeod, Todd	Fresno City College
Kern-Blystone, Dorothy Jean	Bowling Green State	McManus, Illyana	Grossmont College
		McPherson, Dori	Schoolcraft College
Keskin, Ilknur	The University of South Dakota	Meiklejohn, Nancy	Pikes Peak Community College
Kirk, Colleen	Mercy College	Menking, Rick	Hardin-Simmons University
Kleckner, Michelle	Elon University	Meredith, Mary	University of Louisiana at Lafayette
Kliston, Linda	Broward Community College, North Campus	Mermelstein, Lisa	Baruch College
		Metos, Linda	Salt Lake Community College
Kochis, Dennis	Suffolk County Community College	Meurer, Daniel	University of Cincinnati
Kramer, Ed	Northern Virginia Community College	Meyer, Marian	Central New Mexico Community College
Laird, Jeff	Northeast State Community College	Miller, Cindy	Ivy Tech Community College, Lafayette, Indiana
Lamoureaux, Jackie	Central New Mexico Community College		
		Mitchell, Susan	Davenport University
Lange, David	Grand Valley State	Mohle, Dennis	Fresno Community College
LaPointe, Deb	Central New Mexico Community College	Monk, Ellen	University of Delaware
		Moore, Rodney	Holland College
Larson, Donna	Louisville Technical Institute	Morris, Mike	Southeastern Oklahoma State University
Laspina, Kathy	Vance-Granville Community College		
Le Grand, Dr. Kate	Broward Community College	Morris, Nancy	Hudson Valley Community College
Lenhart, Sheryl	Terra Community College	Moseler, Dan	Harrisburg Area Community College
Letavec, Chris	University of Cincinnati	Nabors, Brent	Reedley College, Clovis Center
Liefert, Jane	Everett Community College	Nadas, Erika	Wright College
Lindaman, Linda	Black Hawk Community College	Nadelman, Cindi	New England College
Lindberg, Martha	Minnesota State University	Nademlynsky, Lisa	Johnson & Wales University
Lightner, Renee	Broward Community College	Ncube, Cathy	University of West Florida
Lindberg, Martha	Minnesota State University	Nagengast, Joseph	Florida Career College
Linge, Richard	Arizona Western College	Newsome, Eloise	Northern Virginia Community College Woodbridge
Logan, Mary G.	Delgado Community College		
Loizeaux, Barbara	Westchester Community College	Nicholls, Doreen	Mohawk Valley Community College
Lopez, Don	Clovis-State Center Community College District	Nunan, Karen	Northeast State Technical Community College

Contributors vii

Odegard, Teri — Edmonds Community College
Ogle, Gregory — North Community College
Orr, Dr. Claudia — Northern Michigan University South
Otieno, Derek — DeVry University
Otton, Diana Hill — Chesapeake College
Oxendale, Lucia — West Virginia Institute of Technology

Paiano, Frank — Southwestern College
Patrick, Tanya — Clackamas Community College
Peairs, Deb — Clark State Community College
Prince, Lisa — Missouri State University-Springfield Campus
Proietti, Kathleen — Northern Essex Community College
Pusins, Delores — HCCC
Raghuraman, Ram — Joliet Junior College
Reasoner, Ted Allen — Indiana University—Purdue
Reeves, Karen — High Point University
Remillard, Debbie — New Hampshire Technical Institute
Rhue, Shelly — DeVry University
Richards, Karen — Maplewoods Community College
Richardson, Mary — Albany Technical College
Rodgers, Gwen — Southern Nazarene University
Roselli, Diane — Harrisburg Area Community College
Ross, Dianne — University of Louisiana in Lafayette
Rousseau, Mary — Broward Community College, South
Samson, Dolly — Hawaii Pacific University
Sams, Todd — University of Cincinnati
Sandoval, Everett — Reedley College
Sardone, Nancy — Seton Hall University
Scafide, Jean — Mississippi Gulf Coast Community College
Scheeren, Judy — Westmoreland County Community College
Schneider, Sol — Sam Houston State University
Scroggins, Michael — Southwest Missouri State University
Sever, Suzanne — Northwest Arkansas Community College
Sheridan, Rick — California State University-Chico
Silvers, Pamela — Asheville Buncombe Tech
Singer, Steven A. — University of Hawai'i, Kapi'olani Community College
Sinha, Atin — Albany State University
Skolnick, Martin — Florida Atlantic University
Smith, T. Michael — Austin Community College
Smith, Tammy — Tompkins Cortland Community Collge
Smolenski, Bob — Delaware County Community College
Spangler, Candice — Columbus State
Stedham, Vicki — St. Petersburg College, Clearwater
Stefanelli, Greg — Carroll Community College
Steiner, Ester — New Mexico State University
Stenlund, Neal — Northern Virginia Community College, Alexandria
St. John, Steve — Tulsa Community College

Sterling, Janet — Houston Community College
Stoughton, Catherine — Laramie County Community College
Sullivan, Angela — Joliet Junior College
Szurek, Joseph — University of Pittsburgh at Greensburg
Tarver, Mary Beth — Northwestern State University
Taylor, Michael — Seattle Central Community College
Thangiah, Sam — Slippery Rock University
Thompson-Sellers, Ingrid — Georgia Perimeter College
Tomasi, Erik — Baruch College
Toreson, Karen — Shoreline Community College
Trifiletti, John J. — Florida Community College at Jacksonville
Trivedi, Charulata — Quinsigamond Community College, Woodbridge
Tucker, William — Austin Community College
Turgeon, Cheryl — Asnuntuck Community College
Turpen, Linda — Central New Mexico Community College
Upshaw, Susan — Del Mar College
Unruh, Angela — Central Washington University
Vanderhoof, Dr. Glenna — Missouri State University-Springfield Campus
Vargas, Tony — El Paso Community College
Vicars, Mitzi — Hampton University
Villarreal, Kathleen — Fresno
Vitrano, Mary Ellen — Palm Beach Community College
Volker, Bonita — Tidewater Community College
Wahila, Lori (Mindy) — Tompkins Cortland Community College
Waswick, Kim — Southeast Community College, Nebraska
Wavle, Sharon — Tompkins Cortland Community College
Webb, Nancy — City College of San Francisco
Wells, Barbara E. — Central Carolina Technical College
Wells, Lorna — Salt Lake Community College
Welsh, Jean — Lansing Community College Nebraska
White, Bruce — Quinnipiac University
Willer, Ann — Solano Community College
Williams, Mark — Lane Community College
Wilson, Kit — Red River College
Wilson, Roger — Fairmont State University
Wimberly, Leanne — International Academy of Design and Technology
Worthington, Paula — Northern Virginia Community College
Yauney, Annette — Herkimer County Community College
Yip, Thomas — Passaic Community College
Zavala, Ben — Webster Tech
Zlotow, Mary Ann — College of DuPage
Zudeck, Steve — Broward Community College, North

About the Authors

Shelley Gaskin, Series Editor, is a professor of business and computer technology at Pasadena City College in Pasadena, California. She holds a master's degree in business education from Northern Illinois University and a doctorate in adult and community education from Ball State University. Dr. Gaskin has 15 years of experience in the computer industry with several Fortune 500 companies and has developed and written training materials for custom systems applications in both the public and private sector. She is also the author of books on Microsoft Outlook and word processing.

Robert L. Ferrett recently retired as the director of the Center for Instructional Computing at Eastern Michigan University, where he provided computer training and support to faculty. He has authored or co-authored more than 70 books on Access, PowerPoint, Excel, Publisher, WordPerfect, and Word. Before writing for the *GO! Series*, Bob was a series editor and author for the *Learn Series*. He has a bachelor's degree in psychology, a master's degree in geography, and a master's degree in interdisciplinary technology from Eastern Michigan University. Bob's doctoral studies were in instructional technology at Wayne State University. For fun, Bob teaches a four-week computers and genealogy class and has written genealogy and local history books.

Visual Walk-Through of the *GO!* System

The *GO!* System is designed for ease of implementation on the instructor side and ease of understanding on the student. It has been completely developed based on professor and student feedback.

The *GO!* System is divided into three categories that reflect how you might organize your course—**Prepare**, **Teach**, and **Assess**.

Prepare

GO!

Because the GO! System was designed and written by instructors like yourself, it includes the tools that allow you to Prepare, Teach, and Assess in your course. We have organized the GO! System into these three categories that match how you work through your course and thus, it's even easier for you to implement.

To help you get started, here is an outline of the first activities you may want to do in order to conduct your course.

There are several other tools not listed here that are available in the GO! System so please refer to your GO! Guide for a complete listing of all the tools.

Prepare
1. Prepare the course syllabus
2. Plan the course assignments
3. Organize the student resources

Teach
4. Conduct demonstrations and lectures

Assess
5. Assign and grade assignments, quizzes, tests, and assessments

PREPARE

1. Prepare the course syllabus
A syllabus template is provided on the IRCD in the **go07_syllabus_template** folder of the main directory. It includes a course calendar planner for 8-week, 12-week, and 16-week formats. Depending on your term (summer or regular semester) you can modify one of these according to your course plan, and then add information pertinent to your course and institution.

2. Plan course assignments
For each chapter, an Assignment Sheet listing every in-chapter and end-of-chapter project is located on the IRCD within the **go01_go!office2007intro_instructor_resources_by_chapter** folder. From there, navigate to the specific chapter folder. These sheets are Word tables, so you can delete rows for the projects that you choose not to assign or add rows for your own assignments—if any. There is a column to add the number of points you want to assign to each project depending on your grading scheme. At the top of the sheet, you can fill in the course information.

Transitioning to GO! Office 2007   Page 1 of 1

NEW

Transition Guide

New to *GO!*—We've made it quick and easy to plan the format and activities for your class.

GO! with Microsoft Office 2007 Introductory
SAMPLE SYLLABUS (16 weeks)

I. COURSE INFORMATION

Course No.:	Semester:
Course Title:	Credits:
Course Hours:	

Instructor:	Office:
Office Hours:	
Email:	Phone:

II. TEXT AND MATERIALS
Before starting the course, you will need the following:

➤ GO! with Microsoft Office 2007 Introductory by Shelley Gaskin, Robert L. Ferrett, Alicia Vargas, Suzanne Marks ©2007, published by Pearson Prentice Hall.
ISBN 0-13-167990-6

➤ Storage device for saving files (any of the following: multiple diskettes, CD-RW, flash drive, etc.)

III. WHAT YOU WILL LEARN IN THIS COURSE
This is a hands-on course where you will learn to use a computer to practice the most commonly used Microsoft programs including the Windows operating system, Internet Explorer for navigating the Internet, Outlook for managing your personal information and the four most popular programs within the Microsoft Office Suite (Word, Excel, PowerPoint and Access). You will also practice the basics of using a computer, mouse and keyboard. You will learn to be an intermediate level user of the Microsoft Office Suite.

Within the Microsoft Office Suite, you will use Word, Excel, PowerPoint, and Access. Microsoft Word is a word processing program with which you can create common business and personal documents. Microsoft Excel is a spreadsheet program that organizes and calculates accounting-type information. Microsoft PowerPoint is a presentation graphics program with which you can develop slides to accompany an oral presentation. Finally, Microsoft Access is a database program that organizes large amounts of information in a useful manner.

Syllabus Template

Includes course calendar planner for 8-,12-, and 16-week formats.

Assignment Sheet

One per chapter. Lists all possible assignments; add to and delete from this simple Word table according to your course plan.

File Guide to the *GO!* Supplements

Tabular listing of all supplements and their file names.

NEW

Assignment Planning Guide

Description of *GO!* assignments with recommendations based on class size, delivery mode, and student needs. Includes examples from fellow instructors.

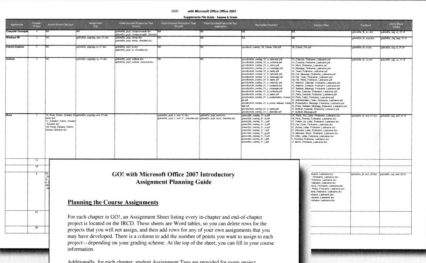

GO! with Microsoft Office 2007 Introductory
Assignment Planning Guide

Planning the Course Assignments

For each chapter in GO!, an Assignment Sheet listing every in-chapter and end-of-chapter project is located on the IRCD. These sheets are Word tables, so you can delete rows for the projects that you will not assign, and then add rows for any of your own assignments that you may have developed. There is a column to add the number of points you want to assign to each project—depending on your grading scheme. At the top of the sheet, you can fill in your course information.

Additionally, for each chapter, student Assignment Tags are provided for every project (including Problem Solving projects)—also located on the IRCD. These are small scoring checklists on which you can check off errors made by the student, and with which the student can verify that all project elements are complete. For campus classes, the student can attach the tags to his or her paper submissions. For online classes, many GO! instructors have the student include these with the electronic submission.

Deciding What to Assign

Front Portion of the Chapter—Instructional Projects: The projects in the front portion of the chapter, which are listed on the first page of each chapter, are the instructional projects. Most instructors assign all of these projects, because this is where the student receives the instruction and engages in the active learning.

End-of-Chapter—Practice and Critical Thinking Projects: In the back portion of the chapter (the gray pages), you can assign on a prescriptive basis; that is, for students who were challenged by the instructional projects, you might assign one or more projects from the two *Skills Reviews*, which provide maximum prompting and a thorough review of the entire chapter. For students who have previous software knowledge and who completed the instructional projects easily, you might assign only the *Mastery Projects*.

You can also assign prescriptively by Objective, because each end-of-chapter project indicates the Objectives covered. So you might assign, on a student-by-student basis, only the projects that cover the Objectives with which the student seemed to have difficulty in the instructional projects.

The five Problem Solving projects and the You and GO! project are the authentic assessments that pull together the student's learning. Here the student is presented with a "messy real-life situation" and then uses his or her knowledge and skill to solve a problem, produce a product, give a presentation, or demonstrate a procedure. You might assign one or more of the Problem

GO! Assignment Planning Guide   Page 1 of 1

Student Data Files

Online Study Guide for Students
Interactive objective-style questions based on chapter content.

PowerPoint Slides

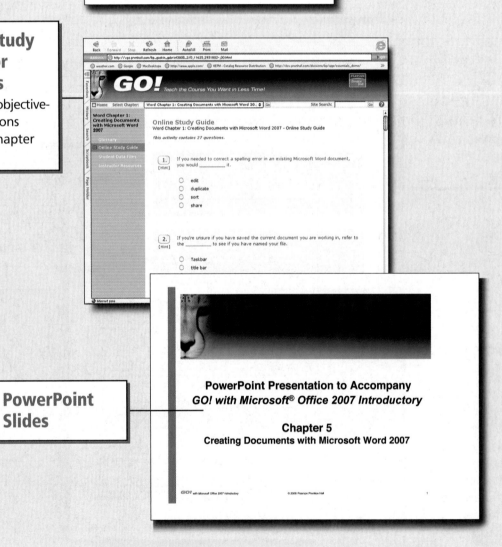

Teach

Student Textbook

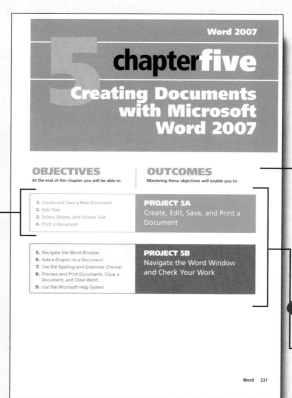

Word 2007

5 chapter five
Creating Documents with Microsoft Word 2007

OBJECTIVES
At the end of this chapter you will be able to:

1. Create and Save a New Document
2. Edit Text
3. Select, Delete, and Format Text
4. Print a Document

5. Navigate the Word Window
6. Add a Graphic to a Document
7. Use the Spelling and Grammar Checker
8. Preview and Print Documents, Close a Document, and Close Word
9. Use the Microsoft Help System

OUTCOMES
Mastering these objectives will enable you to:

PROJECT 5A
Create, Edit, Save, and Print a Document

PROJECT 5B
Navigate the Word Window and Check Your Work

Word 237

Learning Objectives and Student Outcomes

Objectives are clustered around projects that result in student outcomes. They help students learn how to solve problems, not just learn software features.

Project-Based Instruction

Students do not practice features of the application; they create real projects that they will need in the real world. Projects are color coded for easy reference and are named to reflect skills the students will be practicing.

NEW

A and B Projects

Each chapter contains two instructional projects—A and B.

Music School Records

Music School Records was created to launch young musical artists with undiscovered talent in jazz, classical, and contemporary music. The creative management team searches internationally for talented young people, and has a reputation for mentoring and developing the skills of its artists. The company's music is tailored to an audience that is young, knowledgeable about music, and demands the highest quality recordings. Music School Records releases are available in CD format as well as digital downloads.

Getting Started with Microsoft Office Word 2007

A word processor is the most common program found on personal computers and one that almost everyone has a reason to use. When you learn word processing you are also learning skills and techniques that you need to work efficiently on a personal computer. You can use Microsoft Word to perform basic word processing tasks such as writing a memo, a report, or a letter. You can also use Word to complete complex word processing tasks, such as those that include sophisticated tables, embedded graphics, and links to other documents and the Internet. Word is a program that you can learn gradually, and then add more advanced skills one at a time.

Each chapter opens with a story that sets the stage for the projects the student will create; the instruction does not force the student to pretend to be someone or make up a scenario.

Each chapter has an introductory paragraph that briefs students on what is important.

Teach (continued)

Visual Summary
Shows students upfront what their projects will look like when they are done.

Objective
The skills the student will learn are clearly stated at the beginning of each project and color coded to match projects listed on the chapter opener page.

NEW

Screen Shots
Larger screen shots.

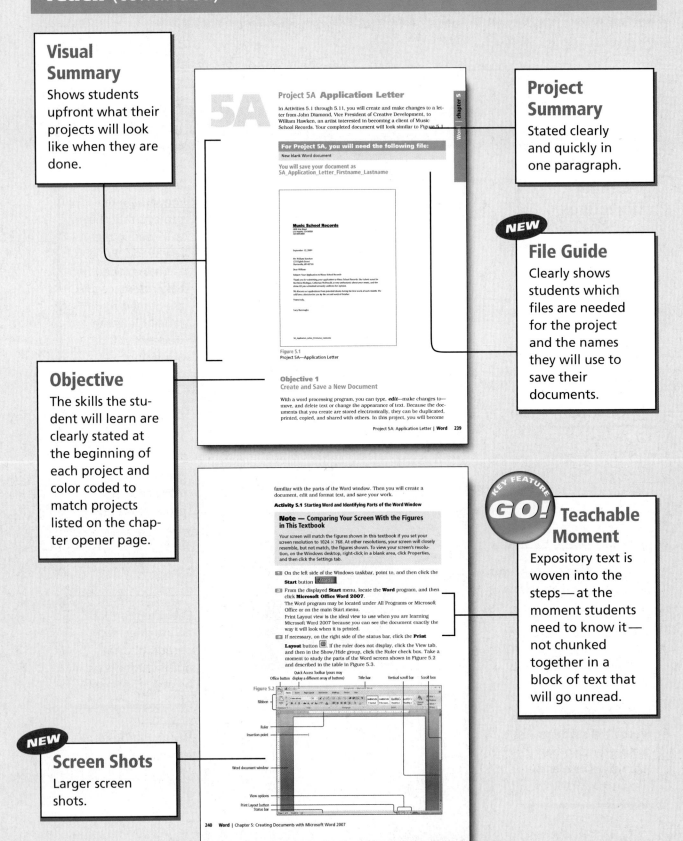

Project Summary
Stated clearly and quickly in one paragraph.

NEW

File Guide
Clearly shows students which files are needed for the project and the names they will use to save their documents.

Teachable Moment
Expository text is woven into the steps—at the moment students need to know it—not chunked together in a block of text that will go unread.

Steps

Color coded to the current project, easy to read, and not too many to confuse the student or too few to be meaningless.

Sequential Pagination

No more confusing letters and abbreviations.

End-of-Project Icon

All projects in the *GO! Series* have clearly identifiable end points, useful in self-paced or on-line environments.

Microsoft Procedural Syntax

All steps are written in Microsoft Procedural Syntax to put the student in the right place at the right time.

Press [Enter] two more times.

In a business letter, insert two blank lines between the date and the inside address, which is the same as the address you would use on an envelope.

Type **Mr. William Hawken** and then press [Enter].

The wavy red line under the proper name *Hawken* indicates that the word has been flagged as misspelled because it is a word not contained in the Word dictionary.

On two lines, type the following address, but do not press [Enter] at the end of the second line:

123 Eighth Street
Harrisville, MI 48740

Note — Typing the Address

Include a comma after the city name in an inside address. However, for mailing addresses on envelopes, eliminate the comma after the city name.

On the **Home tab**, in the **Styles group**, click the **Normal** button.

The Normal style is applied to the text in the rest of the document. Recall that the Normal style adds extra space between paragraphs; it also adds slightly more space between lines in a paragraph.

Press [Enter]. Type **Dear William:** and then press [Enter].

This salutation is the line that greets the person receiving the letter.

Type **Subject: Your Application to Music School Records** and press [Enter]. Notice the light dots between words, which indicate spaces and display when formatting marks are displayed. Also, notice the extra space after each paragraph, and then compare your screen with Figure 5.6.

The subject line is optional, but you should include a subject line in most letters to identify the topic. Depending on your Word settings, a wavy green line may display in the subject line, indicating a potential grammar error.

Note — Space Between Lines in Your Printed Document

The Cambria font, and many others, uses a slightly larger space between the lines than more traditional fonts like Times New Roman. As you progress in your study of Word, you will use many different fonts and also adjust the spacing between lines.

From the **Office** menu, click **Close**, saving any changes if prompted to do so. Leave Word open for the next project.

Another Way | **To Print a Document**

To Print a document:

- From the Office menu, click Print to display the Print dialog box (to be covered later), from which you can choose a variety of different options, such as printing multiple copies, printing on a different printer, and printing some but not all pages.
- Hold down [Ctrl] and then press [P]. This is an alternative to the Office menu command, and opens the Print dialog box.
- Hold down [Alt], press [F], and then press [P]. This opens the Print dialog box.

End You have completed Project 5A

Teach (continued)

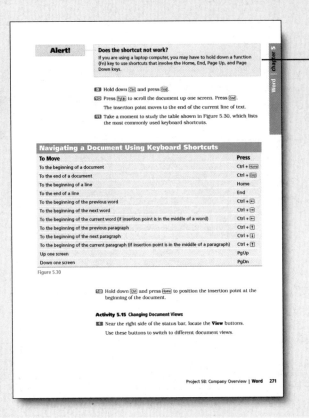

Alert box
Draws students' attention to make sure they aren't getting too far off course.

Another Way box
Shows students other ways of doing tasks.

More Knowledge box
Expands on a topic by going deeper into the material.

Note box
Points out important items to remember.

NEW

There's More You Can Do!
Try IT! exercises that teach students additional skills.

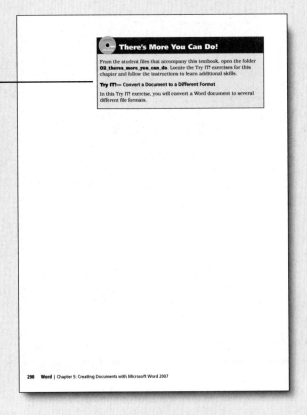

End-of-Chapter Material

Take your pick! Content-based or Outcomes-based projects to choose from. Below is a table outlining the various types of projects that fit into these two categories.

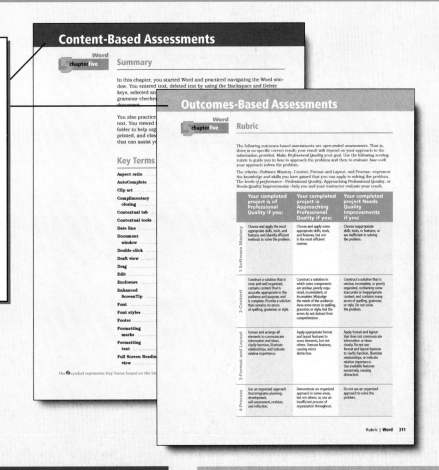

Content-Based Assessments

(Defined solutions with solution files provided for grading)

Project Letter	Name	Objectives Covered
N/A	Summary and Key Terms	
N/A	Multiple Choice	
N/A	Fill-in-the-blank	
C	Skills Review	Covers A Objectives
D	Skills Review	Covers B Objectives
E	Mastering Excel	Covers A Objectives
F	Mastering Excel	Covers B Objectives
G	Mastering Excel	Covers any combination of A and B Objectives
H	Mastering Excel	Covers any combination of A and B Objectives
I	Mastering Excel	Covers all A and B Objectives
J	Business Running Case	Covers all A and B Objectives

Outcomes-Based Assessments

(Open solutions that require a rubric for grading)

Project Letter	Name	Objectives Covered
N/A	Rubric	
K	Problem Solving	Covers as many Objectives from A and B as possible
L	Problem Solving	Covers as many Objectives from A and B as possible.
M	Problem Solving	Covers as many Objectives from A and B as possible.
N	Problem Solving	Covers as many Objectives from A and B as possible.
O	Problem Solving	Covers as many Objectives from A and B as possible.
P	You and GO!	Covers as many Objectives from A and B as possible
Q	GO! Help	Not tied to specific objectives
R	* Group Business Running Case	Covers A and B Objectives

* This project is provided only with the *GO! with Microsoft Office 2007 Introductory* book.

Objectives List

Most projects in the end-of-chapter section begin with a list of the objectives covered.

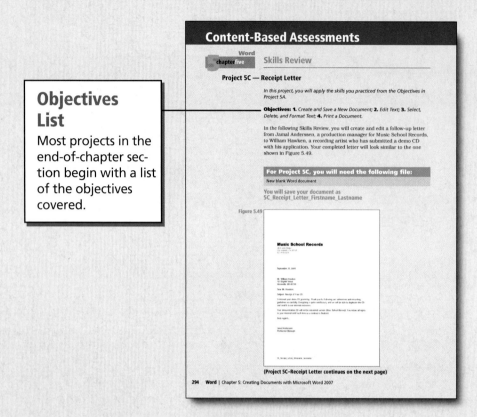

End of Each Project Clearly Marked

Clearly identified end points help separate the end-of-chapter projects.

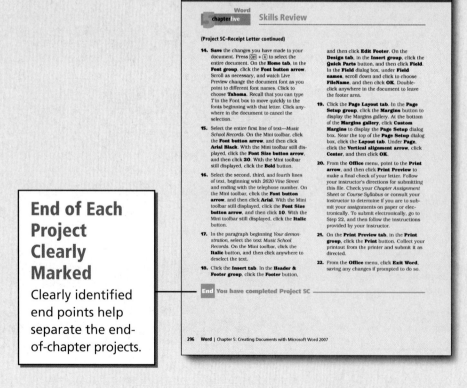

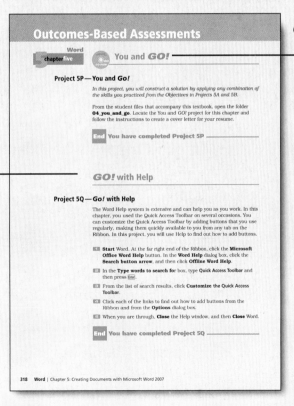

NEW

Rubric

A matrix that states the criteria and standards for grading student work. Used to grade open-ended assessments.

GO! with Help

Students practice using the Help feature of the Office application.

NEW

You and *GO!*

A project in which students use information from their own lives and apply the skills from the chapter to a personal task.

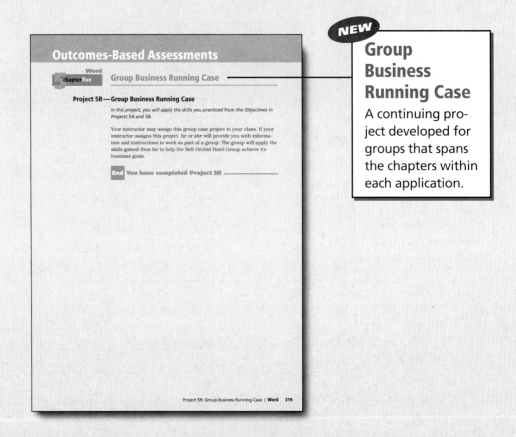

NEW

Group Business Running Case

A continuing project developed for groups that spans the chapters within each application.

Student CD includes:

- Student Data Files
- There's More You Can Do!
- Business Running Case
- You and *GO!*

Companion Web site

An interactive Web site to further student leaning.

Online Study Guide

Interactive objective-style questions to help students study.

Annotated Instructor Edition

The Annotated Instructor Edition contains a full version of the student textbook that includes tips, supplement references, and pointers on teaching with the *GO!* instructional system.

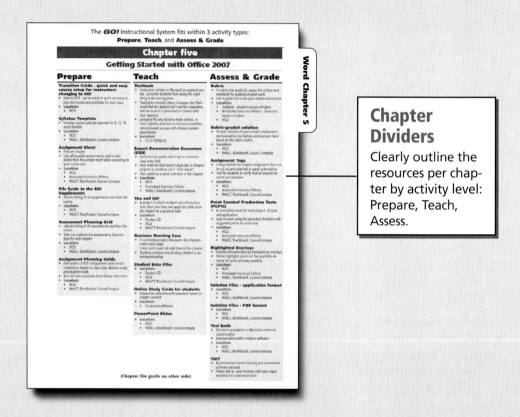

Chapter Dividers

Clearly outline the resources per chapter by activity level: Prepare, Teach, Assess.

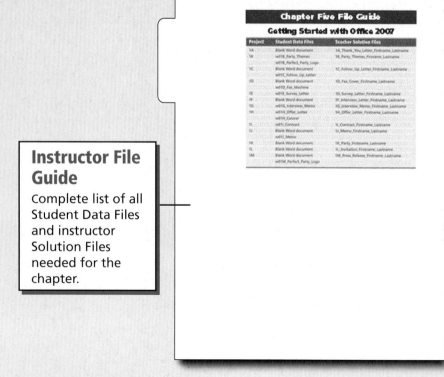

Instructor File Guide

Complete list of all Student Data Files and instructor Solution Files needed for the chapter.

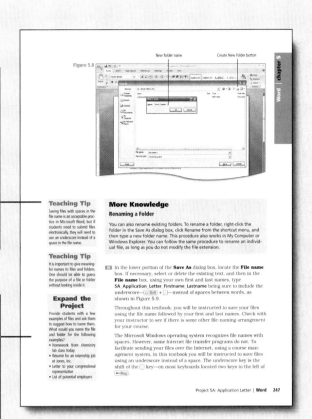

Helpful Hints, Teaching Tips, Expand the Project

References correspond to what is being taught in the student textbook.

NEW

Full-Size Textbook Pages

An instructor copy of the textbook with traditional Instructor Manual content incorporated.

End-of-Chapter Concepts Assessments

contain the answers for quick reference.

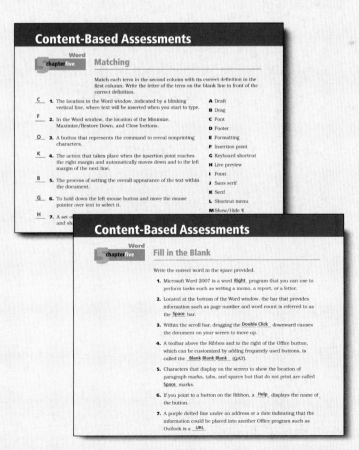

NEW

Rubric

A matrix to guide the student on how they will be assessed is reprinted in the Annotated Instructor Edition with suggested weights for each of the criteria and levels of performance. Instructors can modify the weights to suit their needs.

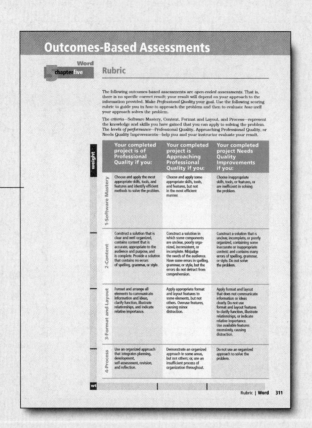

Assignment Tags

NEW

Scoring checklist for assignments. Now also available for Problem-Solving projects.

GO! with Microsoft® Office 2007

Assignment Tags for GO! with Office 2007
Word Chapter 5

Name:				Name:			
Professor:	Project: 5A			Professor:	Project: 5B		
	Course:				Course:		
Task	Points	Your Score		Task	Points	Your Score	
Center text vertically on page	2			Insert the file w05B_Music_School_Records	4		
Delete the word "really"	1			Insert the Music Logo	4		
Delete the words "try to"	1			Remove duplicate "and"	2		
Replace "last" with "first"	1			Change spelling and grammar errors (4)	8		
Insert the word "potential"	1			Correct/Add footer as instructed	2		
Replace "John W. Diamond" with "Lucy Burrows"	2			Circled information is incorrect or formatted incorrectly			
Change entire document to the Cambria font	2						
Change the first line of text to Arial Black 20 pt. font	2						
Bold the first line of text	2						
Change the 2nd through 4th lines to Arial 10 pt.	2						
Italicize the 2nd through 4th lines of text	2						
Correct/Add footer as instructed	2						
Circled information is incorrect or formatted incorrectly							
Total Points	**20**	**0**		**Total Points**	**20**	**0**	

Name:				Name:			
Professor:	Project: 5C			Professor:	Project: 5D		
	Course:				Course:		
Task	Points	Your Score		Task	Points	Your Score	
Add four line letterhead	2			Insert the file w05D_Marketing	4		
Insert today's date	1			Bold the first two title lines	2		
Add address block, subject line, and greeting	2			Correct spelling of "Marketting"	2		
Add two-paragraph body of letter	2			Correct spelling of "geners"	2		
Add closing, name, and title	2			Correct all misspellings of "allready"	2		
In subject line, capitalize "receipt"	1			Correct grammar error "are" to "is"	2		
Change "standards" to "guidelines"	1			Insert the Piano image	4		
Insert "quite"	1			Correct/add footer as instructed	2		
Insert "all"	1			Circled information is incorrect or formatted incorrectly			
Change the first line of text to Arial Black 20 pt. font	2						
Bold the first line of text	1						
Change the 2nd through 4th lines to Arial 10 pt.	1						
Italicize the 2nd through 4th lines of text	1						
Correct/add footer as instructed	2						
Circled information is incorrect or formatted incorrectly							
Total Points	**20**	**0**		**Total Points**	**20**	**0**	

Highlighted Overlays

Solution files provided as transparency overlays. Yellow highlights point out the gradable elements for quick and easy grading.

Music School Records

2620 Vine Street
Los Angeles, CA 90028
323-555-0028

20 point Arial Black, bold and underline

10 point Arial, italic

September 12, 2009

Mr. William Hawken
123 Eighth Street
Harrisville, MI 48740

Text vertically centered on page

Body of document changed to Cambria font, 11 point

Dear William:

Subject: Your Application to Music School Records

Thank you for submitting your application to Music School Records. Our talent scout for Northern Michigan, Catherine McDonald, is very enthusiastic about your music, and the demo CD you submitted certainly confirms her opinion.

Word "really" deleted

We discuss our applications from potential clients during the first week of each month. We will have a decision for you by the second week of October.

Yours Truly,

Words "try to" deleted

Lucy Burroughs

Point-Counted Production Tests (PCPTs)

A cumulative exam for each **project**, **chapter**, and **application**. Easy to score using the provided checklist with suggested points for each task.

GO! with Microsoft® Office 2007 Introductory

Point-Counted Production Test—Project for GO! with Microsoft® Office 2007 Introductory Project 5A

Instructor Name: _____
Course Information: _____

1. Start Word 2007 to begin a new blank document. Save your document as 5A_Cover_Letter_Firstname_Lastname Remember to save your file frequently as you work.

2. If necessary, display the formatting marks. With the insertion point blinking in the upper left corner of the document to the left of the default first paragraph mark, type the current date (you can use AutoComplete).

3. Press Enter three times and type the inside address:

   Music School Records
   2620 Vine Street
   Los Angeles, CA 90028

4. Press Enter three times, and type Dear Ms. Burroughs:

   Press Enter twice, and type Subject: Application to Music School Records

   Press Enter twice, and type the following text (skipping one line between paragraphs):

   I read about Music School Records in Con Brio magazine and I would like to inquire about the possibility of being represented by your company.

   I am very interested in a career in jazz and am planning to relocate to the Los Angeles area in the very near future. I would be interested in learning more about the company and about available opportunities.

   I was a member of my high school jazz band for three years. In addition, I have been playing in the local coffee shop for the last two years. My demo CD, which is enclosed, contains three of my most requested songs.

   I would appreciate the opportunity to speak with you. Thank you for your time and consideration. I look forward to speaking with you about this exciting opportunity.

5. Press Enter three times, and type the closing Sincerely, Press enter four times, and type your name.

6. Insert a footer that contains the file name.

7. Delete the first instance of the word *very* in the second body paragraph, and insert the word modern in front of *jazz*.

Test Bank

Available as TestGen Software or as a Word document for customization.

Chapter 5: Creating Documents with Microsoft Word 2007

Multiple Choice:

1. With word processing programs, how are documents stored?

   A. On a network

   B. On the computer

   C. Electronically

   D. On the floppy disk

   Answer: C   **Reference:** Objective 1: Create and Save a New Document   **Difficulty:** Moderate

2. Because you will see the document as it will print, _____ view is the ideal view to use when learning Microsoft Word 2007.

   A. Reading

   B. Normal

   C. Print Layout

   D. Outline

   Answer: C   **Reference:** Objective 1: Create and Save a New Document   **Difficulty:** Moderate

3. The blinking vertical line where text or graphics will be inserted is called the:

   A. cursor.

   B. insertion point.

   C. blinking line.

   D. I-beam.

   Answer: B   **Reference:** Objective 1: Create and Save a New Document   **Difficulty:** Easy

**Solution Files–
Application
and PDF
format**

Music School Records

Music School Records discovers, launches, and develops the careers of young artists in classical, jazz, and contemporary music. Our philosophy is to not only shape, distribute, and sell a music product, but to help artists create a career that can last a lifetime. Too often in the music industry, artists are forced to fit their music to a trend that is short-lived. Music School Records does not just follow trends, we take a long-term view of the music industry and help our artists develop a style and repertoire that is fluid and flexible and that will appeal to audiences for years and even decades.

The music industry is constantly changing, but over the last decade, the changes have been enormous. New forms of entertainment such as DVDs, video games, and the Internet mean there is more competition for the leisure dollar in the market. New technologies give consumers more options for buying and listening to music, and they are demanding high quality recordings. Young consumers are comfortable with technology and want the music they love when and where they want it, no matter where they are or what they are doing.

Music School Records embraces new technologies and the sophisticated market of young music lovers. We believe that providing high quality recordings of truly talented artists make for more discerning listeners who will cherish the gift of music for the rest of their lives. The expertise of Music School Records includes:

- Insight into our target market and the ability to reach the desired audience
- The ability to access all current sources of music income
- A management team with years of experience in music commerce
- Innovative business strategies and artist development plans
- Investment in technology infrastructure for high quality recordings and business services

pagexxxix_top.docx

Online Assessment and Training

myitlab is Prentice Hall's new performance-based solution that allows you to easily deliver outcomes-based courses on Microsoft Office 2007, with customized training and defensible assessment. Key features of myitlab include:

A *true* "system" approach: myitlab content is the same as in your textbook.
Project-based *and* skills-based: Students complete real-life assignments.
Advanced reporting *and* gradebook: These include student click stream data.
***No* installation required:** myitlab is completely Web-based. You just need an Internet connection, small plug-in, and Adobe Flash Player.

Ask your Prentice Hall sales representative for a demonstration or visit:

www.prenhall.com/myitlab

chapterone

Getting Started with Windows Vista

OBJECTIVES

At the end of this chapter you will be able to:

1. Get Started with Windows Vista
2. Use the Start Menu and Manage Windows
3. Resize, Move, and Scroll Windows

4. Create, Move, and Rename Folders
5. Copy, Move, Rename, and Delete Files
6. Find Files and Folders
7. Use Vista Help

OUTCOMES

Mastering these objectives will enable you to:

Project 1A
Familiarize Yourself with the Vista Interface

Project 1B
Work with Files and Folders

Windows Vista is the software that coordinates the activities of your computer's hardware. Windows Vista controls how your screen is displayed; how you open and close programs; and the startup, shutdown, and navigation procedures for your computer. It is useful to become familiar with the basic features of the Windows Vista operating system, especially working with the Start button and taskbar; opening, closing, moving, and resizing windows; and saving and managing files.

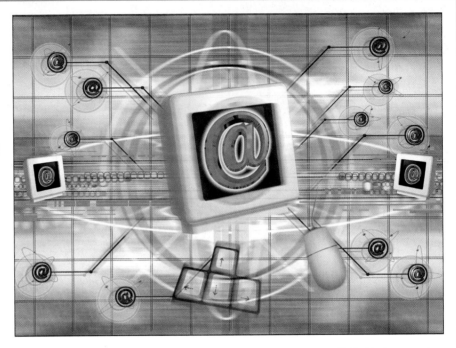

© Getty Images, Inc.

Getting Started with Windows Vista

Project 1A Familiarize Yourself with the Vista Interface

In Activities 1.1 through 1.9, you will explore the Windows Vista screen and practice navigating Windows Vista. You will open, close, resize, and move windows, and you will open several windows at one time. The screens that you will be working with will look similar to Figure 1.1.

For Project 1A, you will need the following files:

No files needed for this project

Figure 1.1
Project 1A—Familiarize Yourself with the Vista Interface

Objective 1
Get Started with Windows Vista

Windows Vista is an *operating system*—software that controls the *hardware* attached to your computer, including its memory, disk drive space, attached devices such as printers and scanners, and the central processing unit. Windows Vista and earlier versions of Windows are similar; they use a *graphical user interface (GUI)*. A GUI uses graphics or pictures to represent commands and actions and enables you to see document formatting on the screen as it will look when printed on paper. *Windows*, when spelled with a capital *W*, refers to the operating system that runs your computer.

Starting Windows is an automatic procedure; you turn on your computer, and after a few moments the version of Windows installed on your computer displays. Some versions require that you log in, and some do not. If you are using a different version of Windows, some procedures used in this chapter may work differently. Windows Vista is available in several editions: Home Basic, Home Premium, Business, and Ultimate. For large institutions, there is also an Enterprise edition. For most tasks, the Home Premium, Business, and Ultimate editions work the same. The Business edition, however, does not support many multimedia features.

Alert!

Does your screen differ?

This chapter uses Windows Vista Home Premium Edition, and there are some differences between the look of this edition and the other editions. More importantly, the look of the screen will depend largely on the setting options that have been selected for your computer, and on the type of hardware installed in your computer—especially the video card and memory.

Activity 1.1 Exploring the Windows Vista Screen

In this activity, you will examine the different components of the Windows Vista screen.

1 Turn on your computer and wait for the **Windows** program to display, or follow the log-on instructions required for the computer you are using. For example, you might have to click a name on a Welcome screen, or enter a user ID or password. If this is your home computer and you are the only user, it is likely that you need do nothing except wait for a few moments. If you see the Welcome Center screen, examine its contents, and when you are done, click the red button with the X in the upper right corner of the window.

The Windows *desktop*, which is the working area of the Windows Vista screen, displays. The working area is called a desktop because on it you can place electronic versions of things you have on your regular desk. The screen look will vary, depending on which version of Windows you are using and what you have on your own desktop.

Note — The Welcome Center

The **Welcome Center** window displays links to a number of topics, including upgrading Windows, connecting to the Internet, adding new users, and taking advantage of special offers from Microsoft. By default, the Welcome Center window displays every time you start your computer. If you clear the check box at the bottom of the window, you will skip this window at start-up. If your Welcome Center does not display, and you would like to take advantage of any of its features, click the Start button, and then click Welcome Center.

2 Compare your Windows desktop with Figure 1.2 and then take a moment to study the Windows elements identified in the table in Figure 1.3.

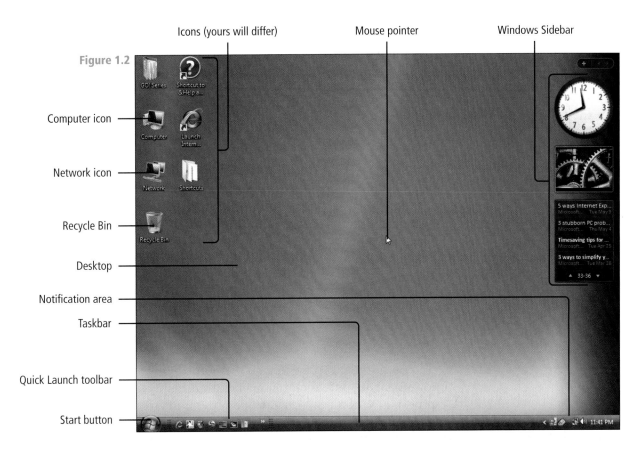

Figure 1.2

Icons (yours will differ) Mouse pointer Windows Sidebar

Computer icon
Network icon
Recycle Bin
Desktop
Notification area
Taskbar
Quick Launch toolbar
Start button

Windows Screen Elements

Screen Element	Description
Computer icon	An icon that represents the computer on which you are working, and that provides access to the drives, folders, and files on your computer.
Desktop	The working area of the Windows Vista screen, consisting of program icons, a taskbar, a Sidebar, and a Start button.
Icon	A graphic representation of an object that you can select and open, such as a drive, a disk, a folder, a document, or a program.

(Continued)

(Continued)

Mouse pointer	The arrow, I-beam, or other symbol that moves when you move the mouse or other pointing device, and that indicates a location or position on your screen—also called the *pointer*.
Network icon	An icon that represents the network to which your computer is attached, and that provides access to the drives, folders, and files on your network.
Notification area	The area on the right side of the taskbar, formerly called the *system tray* or *status area*, where the clock and system notifications display. These notifications keep you informed about the processes that are occurring in the background, such as antivirus software checking, network connections, and other utility programs. Some notifications display only temporarily.
Quick Launch toolbar	An area to the right of the Start button that contains shortcut icons for commonly used programs.
Recycle Bin	A temporary storage area for files that you have deleted. Files can be either recovered or permanently removed from the Recycle Bin.
Start button	The button on the left side of the taskbar that is used to start programs, change system settings, find Windows help, or shut down the computer.
Taskbar	Displays the Start button and the name of any open documents. The taskbar may also display shortcut buttons for other programs.
Windows Sidebar	An area on the right side of the screen that displays useful gadgets, such as a clock, a stock market ticker, or a weather map.

Figure 1.3

3 Move the mouse across a flat surface to move the pointer on your screen. On the desktop, position the tip of the pointer in the center of the **Computer** icon—an action referred to as *pointing*. *Double-click*—press the left mouse button two times in rapid succession—using caution not to move the mouse. If the Computer icon is not visible, click Start, and then from the right side of the displayed Start menu, click Computer. Compare your screen with Figure 1.4, and then take a moment to study the **Computer** window elements in the table Figure 1.5.

The Computer window displays. A *window*—spelled with a lowercase *w*—is a rectangular box that displays information or a program. When a window is open, the name of the window is displayed—either in the status bar or in the title bar—and on a button on the taskbar at the bottom of the desktop.

Alert!

Does your screen differ?
Because the configuration of your Computer window depends on how it was last used, your window may not display all of the elements shown in Figure 1.4, in particular the menu bar, Details pane, Folders list, and Search box. Also, your Computer window may cover the entire screen.

Figure 1.4

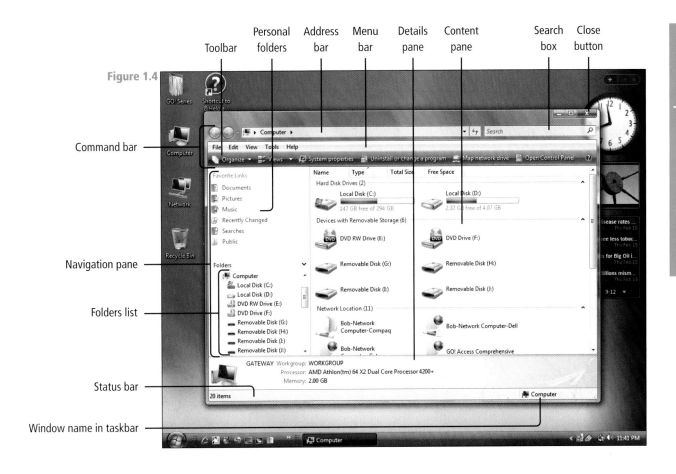

Labels around figure:
Toolbar
Personal folders
Address bar
Menu bar
Details pane
Content pane
Search box
Close button
Command bar
Navigation pane
Folders list
Status bar
Window name in taskbar

Parts of a Window

Screen Element	Description
Address bar	A toolbar that displays the organizational path to the active file, folder, or window.
Close button	A shortcut button in a title bar that closes a window or a program.
Command bar	Area at the top of a window that includes the toolbar, menu bar, address bar, and search pane.
Content pane	Displays files and folders stored in the disk drive or folder that is currently selected in the Navigation pane.
Details pane	Displays details about the drive, folder, or file that is currently selected in the Content pane.
Folders list	Part of the Navigation pane that displays the drive and folder structure on the computer.
Menu bar	The bar near the top of a window that lists the names of menu categories.
Navigation pane	The pane on the left side of the Computer or Windows Explorer window that contains Personal folders and the Folders list.
Personal folders	The top part of the Navigation pane that displays folders associated with the current user.
ScreenTip	A small box, activated by pointing to a button or other screen object, that displays the name of or further information about the screen element.
Search box	A box in which you type a search word or phrase.

(Continued)

(Continued)

Status bar	A horizontal bar at the bottom of the document window that provides information about the current state of what you are viewing in the window, for example, the page number of a document. In some cases, the status bar also displays the name of the window.
Toolbar	A row of buttons that activate commands with a single click of the left mouse button.
Window name	The name of the window or program, displayed in the window status bar or title bar.

Figure 1.5

4 In the upper right corner of the **Computer** window title bar, point to, but do not click, the **Close** button ![X], and then notice that the ScreenTip *Close* displays.

A **ScreenTip** is a small note, usually in a yellow box, that provides information about or describes a screen element.

5 *Click*—press the left mouse button one time—the **Close** button ![X] to close the **Computer** window. Then, point to the **Computer** icon on the desktop and click the right mouse button—this action is known as a *right-click*. If the Computer icon does not display on your desktop, click the Start button ![icon], and then right-click Computer. Compare your screen with Figure 1.6.

A shortcut menu displays. A **menu** is a list of commands within a category. **Shortcut menus** list **context-sensitive commands**—commands commonly used when working with the selected object. On this shortcut menu, the Open command is displayed in bold because it is the default action that occurs when you double-click this icon.

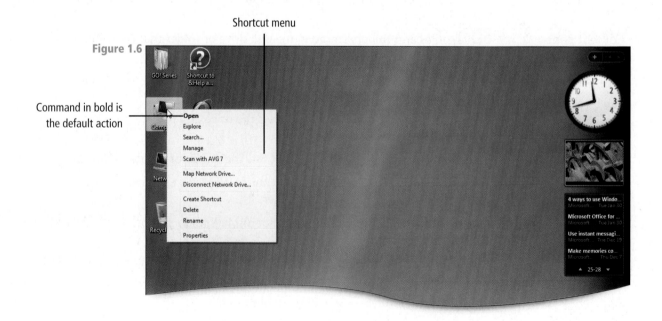

Shortcut menu

Figure 1.6

Command in bold is the default action

6 From the displayed shortcut menu, point to **Open** to highlight—select—the command, and then click one time. In the displayed **Computer** window, near the top of the **Content** pane, point to and then click the disk drive labeled **Local Disk (C:)**, and then notice the **Details** pane. Compare your screen with Figure 1.7.

The specifications of the *Local Disk*—the large disk drive inside your computer system, also referred to as the *hard drive*—are displayed in the Details pane. A *drive* is an area of storage that is formatted with the Windows file system, and that has a drive letter such as C, D, E, and so on.

Window
title

Close
button

Figure 1.7

Drive C: selected

Click to expand or hide
the Folders list

Details of the local disk

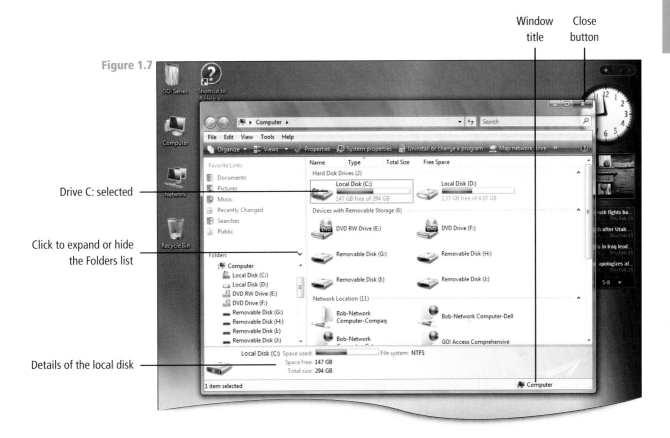

Alert!

Is your Details pane missing?

Recall that the configuration of your Computer window may vary, depending on how it was last configured. If your Details pane does not display, in the toolbar, click Organize, point to Layout, and then click Details Pane.

7 In the **Computer** window title bar, click the **Close** button .

More Knowledge

The Windows Aero User Interface

The screen you see in the figures in this book use the *Windows Aero* user interface. Windows Aero—which is an acronym for *A*uthentic, *E*nergetic, *R*eflective, *O*pen—features a three dimensional look, with transparent window frames, live previews of open windows, and multiple color schemes. This user interface is available with all but the most basic versions of Vista, but requires fairly substantial amounts of memory and powerful video cards. If your screen does not have the same look, your computer may not be capable of displaying the Aero interface.

Activity 1.2 Personalizing the Desktop

The Windows Vista desktop can be personalized to suit your needs and tastes. You can, for example, change the resolution of the monitor to make it easier to read, or to display more information. In this activity, you will change the screen saver and practice changing the desktop background.

1 Move the pointer to an open area of the desktop, and then right-click.

A shortcut menu displays commands that are available for your desktop.

2 From the displayed shortcut menu, move the pointer to the bottom of the list, and then click **Personalize**. Notice that the Personalization window displays, as shown in Figure 1.8.

Figure 1.8

Desktop Background options ——

Screen Saver options ——

Personalization window ——

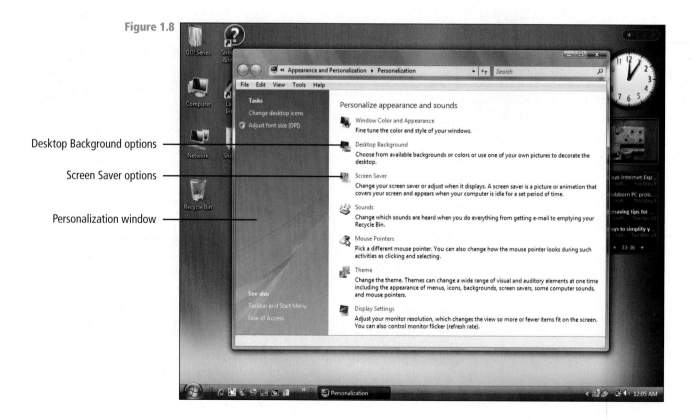

3 In the displayed **Personalization** window, click **Screen Saver**.

A *screen saver* is a picture or animation that displays on your screen after a set period of computer inactivity.

4 In the displayed **Screen Saver Settings** dialog box, click the **Screen saver box arrow**. From the displayed list, click **Aquarium**, and then compare your screen with Figure 1.9.

A *dialog box* is a box that asks you to make a decision about an individual object or topic. The Aquarium screen saver is selected, and a preview displays near the top of the dialog box. The default length of inactivity to trigger the screen saver is 15 minutes.

Figure 1.9

Preview of Aquarium screen saver

Screen saver box arrow

Selected screen saver

Period of inactivity before screen saver displays

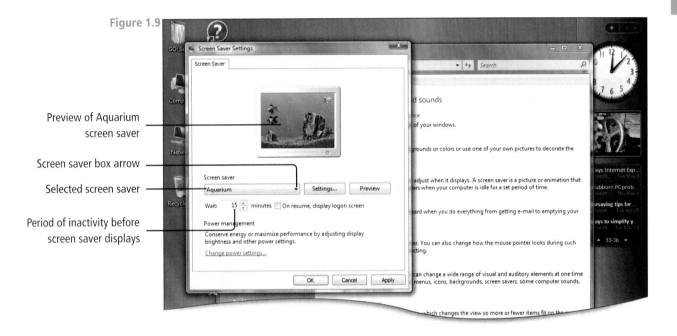

5 In the **Screen Saver Settings** dialog box, click the **Preview** button to preview a full-screen version of the screen saver. When you are through, move the mouse to turn off the screen saver. At the bottom of the dialog box, click **OK**.

6 In the **Personalization** window, click **Desktop Background**.

The *desktop background* is the picture, pattern, or color that displays on the desktop.

7 In the displayed **Desktop Background** window, click the **Picture Location box arrow**, and then from the displayed list, click **Windows Wallpapers**. In the displayed list of desktop backgrounds, under **Light Auras**, click the first background, and then compare your screen with Figure 1.10. If this picture is not available, click another picture.

Windows Wallpaper group

Figure 1.10

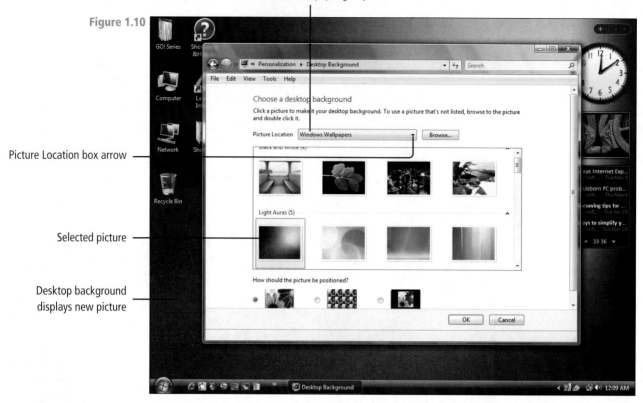

Picture Location box arrow

Selected picture

Desktop background
displays new picture

8 At the bottom of the **Desktop Background** window, click the **Cancel** button.

The Cancel button enables you to leave a window or dialog box without implementing the changes that you have made.

9 In the upper right corner of the **Personalization** window, click the **Close** button ❎.

Activity 1.3 Adding and Removing Gadgets from the Windows Sidebar

The Windows Sidebar is located on the right side of the desktop, and is used to display dynamic programs—also known as *gadgets*—such as a currency converter, a calendar, or a clock. By default, a clock, a picture slideshow, and a news headlines box are displayed; your screen gadgets may be different.

1 In the **Windows Sidebar**, point to the **Clock** gadget. If the Clock gadget does not display, point to any other gadget. Notice that a set of tools displays to the right of the gadget, as shown in Figure 1.11.

The tool set is called the *gadget controls*, and includes a Move button in the shape of eight small dots, an Options button in the shape of a wrench, and a Close button.

Move button   Options button   Gadget controls   Close button

Figure 1.11

Clock gadget

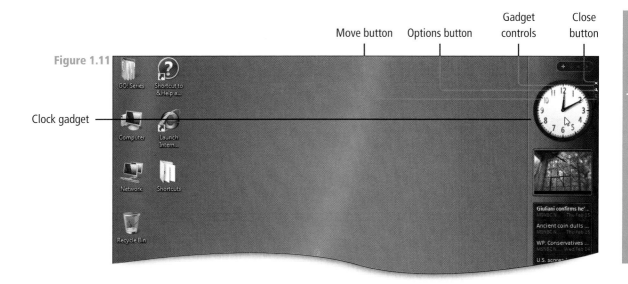

Alert!

Is the Windows Sidebar missing?

If the last person to use the computer turned the Windows Sidebar off, it will remain off until turned back on. To turn on the Windows Sidebar, click the Start button, click All Programs, click Accessories, and then click Windows Sidebar.

2 In the **Windows Sidebar**, right-click in an open area. From the displayed shortcut menu, click **Add Gadgets**. Compare your screen with Figure 1.12.

Note — Removing a Gadget from the Windows Sidebar

To remove a gadget from the Windows Sidebar, right-click the gadget, and then from the displayed shortcut menu, click Close Gadget.

Figure 1.12

Available gadgets

Online link to other gadgets

3 Double-click the **Weather** gadget to place it in the Windows Sidebar. In the upper-right corner of the **Gadgets** dialog box, click the **Close** button [X].

4 Move the pointer over the **Weather** gadget, and then click the **Options** control—the button in the shape of a wrench.

5 In the **Weather** dialog box, click in the **Current Location** box. Type **Madison Wisconsin** and then press [Enter]. Compare your screen with Figure 1.13, and then from the displayed list, click **Madison, Wisconsin**. Under **Current location**, be sure *Madison, Wisconsin* displays.

Weather
dialog box   Selected city

Figure 1.13

6 In the **Weather** dialog box, click **OK** to confirm your selection. Notice that the current temperature and the name of the city display in the weather gadget.

7 If the Feed Headlines gadget does not display, use the techniques you just practiced to add it to the Windows Sidebar. Then, point to the **Feed Headlines** gadget, and click on one of the headlines.

More information displays in a pop-up window. You can click the story headline to see the full article.

8 On the desktop, click in any open area to close the headline.

More Knowledge

Use the Same Gadget More Than One Time

Some of the gadgets can be displayed multiple times. For example, if you are interested in the weather in two different locations, you can add two weather gadgets to the Windows Sidebar and keep an eye on two locations at one time.

Objective 2
Use the Start Menu and Manage Windows

Some programs and documents are available from the desktop. For most things, however, you will turn to the Start menu. The **Start menu** gives you access to all of the programs on your computer, and also enables you to change the way Windows operates, to access and configure your network, and to get help and support when it is needed. Once you have opened several programs, you can rearrange and resize the program windows to fit your needs.

Activity 1.4 Using the Start Menu

In this activity, you will use the Start menu to open an accessory program, and also to open the Computer window.

1 In the lower-left corner of the screen, on the left end of the taskbar, point to and then click the **Start** button 🔵 , and then compare your screen with Figure 1.14. Alternatively, press the Start button on your keyboard—a key with the Windows logo, often found to the left of the spacebar.

The left side of the Start menu contains three areas. At the bottom is the **All Programs** command, which takes you to a list of all of the programs you can access on the computer. Above *All Programs* is an area that contains the most recently opened programs. On the top left is the **pinned programs area**—an area reserved for programs that you want to display permanently, although you can also delete programs from this area. To delete a program from the pinned list, right-click the program, and then click *Remove From This List*.

On the top of the right side are links to your personal folders, while the bottom two sections give you access to many more features. *All Programs* and *Recent Items* display arrows, which indicate that a submenu is available for a command. A **submenu** is a second-level menu; the arrow indicates more items can be found related to the menu command.

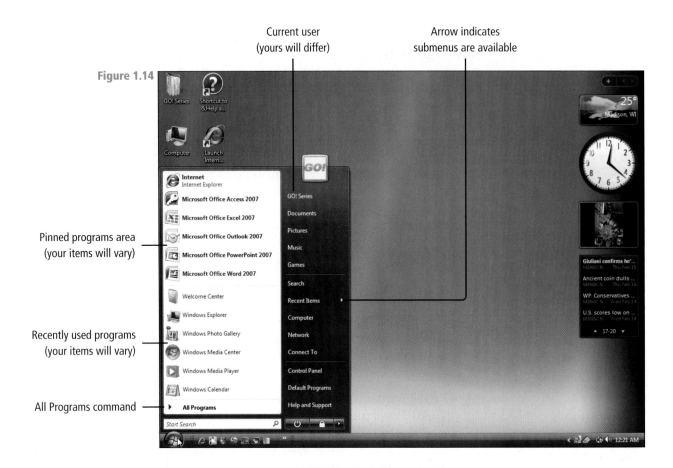

Figure 1.14

Current user
(yours will differ)

Arrow indicates
submenus are available

Pinned programs area
(your items will vary)

Recently used programs
(your items will vary)

All Programs command

Is your taskbar hidden?

Some computers are set up to hide the taskbar when it is not in use. This adds more workspace to the desktop, and is particularly useful on portable computers with small screens. When the taskbar is hidden, move the pointer to the bottom of the screen, and it will display. However, in this chapter, it is assumed that the taskbar is displayed at all times.

To keep the taskbar displayed on your screen, find an open area on the taskbar, right-click, and then from the shortcut menu, click Properties. In the Taskbar and Start Menu Properties dialog box, on the Taskbar tab, locate the *Auto-hide the taskbar* check box. If the taskbar is hidden, there will be a check mark in the check box. To remove the Auto-hide feature, click the check box one time to clear—remove—the check mark. Note: If the Properties dialog box does not display when you right-click, try right-clicking over the clock on the far right side of the taskbar.

2 From the **Start** menu, point to, but do not click, the **All Programs** command. Compare your screen with Figure 1.15.

The All Programs submenu displays—displaying a portion of the contents found within All Programs—and the *All Programs* command changes to a *Back* command. Your menu will differ from the one shown in Figure 1.15 because your computer will have different programs installed. Folders in the menu contain more programs, or more folders, or some of each.

Figure 1.15

Programs

Accessories folder

Folders that contain programs

Back command

▣ Click the **Accessories** folder, and then from the displayed list, click **Calculator**.

The Calculator window opens, and the Start menu closes. You can access the Accessories programs from the Start menu and use them while you are using other programs such as Microsoft Office. For example, you might want to make a quick calculation while you are typing a document in Microsoft Word. You can open the calculator, make the calculation, and then place the result in your Word document without closing Word.

▣ Click the **Start** button 🪟 again, and near the middle of the right side of the **Start menu**, click **Computer**. Compare your screen with Figure 1.16.

The Computer window opens, but the Calculator window is either partially or completely hidden, as shown in Figure 1.16. The buttons in the taskbar, however, indicate that two windows are open, and display the names of the windows. The darker button indicates the ***active window***—the window in which the cursor movements, commands, or text entry occur when two or more windows are open.

Figure 1.16

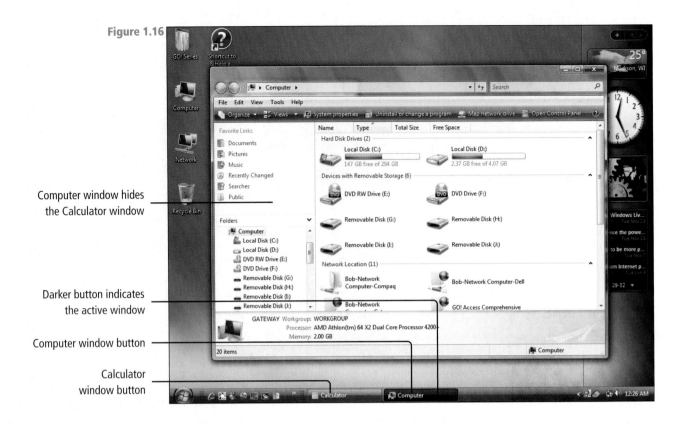

Computer window hides the Calculator window

Darker button indicates the active window

Computer window button

Calculator window button

5. Click the **Start** button 🔵 , click **All Programs**, click **Accessories**, and then click **Welcome Center** to add a third open program to the desktop. Check the taskbar to confirm that three windows are open.

Activity 1.5 Adding Shortcuts to the Start Menu and the Desktop

There are programs that you will seldom use, and there are programs that you will use all the time. To make frequently used programs easily and quickly available, you can pin a shortcut to the program in the Start menu *pinned programs area*, or you can add a shortcut icon to the desktop.

1. Click the **Start** button 🔵 , click **All Programs**, click **Accessories**, and then right-click **Calculator**.

2. From the displayed shortcut menu, click **Pin to Start Menu**. At the bottom of the **Start menu**, click the **Back** button, and notice that *Calculator* has been added to the pinned programs area, as shown in Figure 1.17.

Calculator program
pinned to Start menu

Figure 1.17

Pinned programs area ⟶

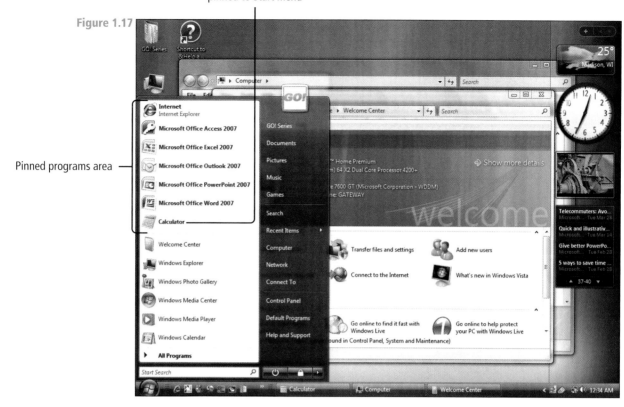

Click the **Start** button , click **All Programs**, click **Accessories**, right-click **Calculator**, and then point to—but do not click—**Send To**. Notice the available commands on the *Send To* list, as shown in Figure 1.18.

Shortcut menu

Desktop (create
shortcut) command

Figure 1.18

Send To command ⟶

Project 1A: Familiarize Yourself with the Vista Interface | **Windows Vista**   **19**

4 From the displayed shortcut menu, click **Desktop (create shortcut)**, and then click in any open area of the desktop. Notice that a Calculator icon is placed on the desktop, as shown in Figure 1.19. Depending on the windows you have open, and the number of icons on your desktop, your Calculator icon may be hidden.

Figure 1.19

Calculator icon added to the desktop

More Knowledge

Resizing the Taskbar

The taskbar can be resized to show more buttons, if necessary. Move the pointer to the top edge of the taskbar until it changes to a two-headed vertical arrow. Hold down the left mouse button and drag up until the taskbar displays all of the buttons for the open windows. You can also shrink the height of the taskbar down to the bottom of the screen. This can be done accidentally, and many new users panic when this happens, thinking the taskbar has disappeared. If you accidentally lose your taskbar, move the pointer to the very bottom of the screen. It will change to a vertical two-headed arrow, and you can drag the top of the taskbar back up to make it visible again.

Activity 1.6 Minimizing, Maximizing, and Restoring a Window

You can **maximize** a window, which enlarges the window to occupy the entire screen, and you can **restore** a window, which reduces the window to the size it was before being maximized. You can also **minimize** a window, which reduces the window to a button on the taskbar, removing it from the screen entirely without actually closing it. When you need to view the window again, you can click the taskbar button to bring it back into view.

1 With the **Welcome Center** window open as the top window, examine the three buttons in the upper right corner of the window. The left button is the **Minimize** button ⬜, the middle button is the **Maximize** button ⬜, and the right button is the **Close** button ✖.

2 In the **Welcome** window, click the **Maximize** button ⬜. Alternatively, double-click in the bar at the top of the window. Notice that the window expands to cover the entire screen, and the Maximize button changes to a Restore Down button ⬜, as shown in Figure 1.20.

Maximize button changes to Restore Down button

Figure 1.20

3 In the **Welcome** window, click the **Restore Down** button ⬜. Alternatively, double-click in the bar at the top of the window. Notice that the window resumes its former shape, size, and location.

4 In the **Welcome** window, click the **Minimize** button ⬜ to display the Computer window. In the **Computer** window, click the **Minimize** button ⬜. Notice that the Calculator window, which had been hidden, now displays. Notice also that the two programs that you minimized are not closed—their buttons still display on the taskbar, as shown in Figure 1.21.

Figure 1.21

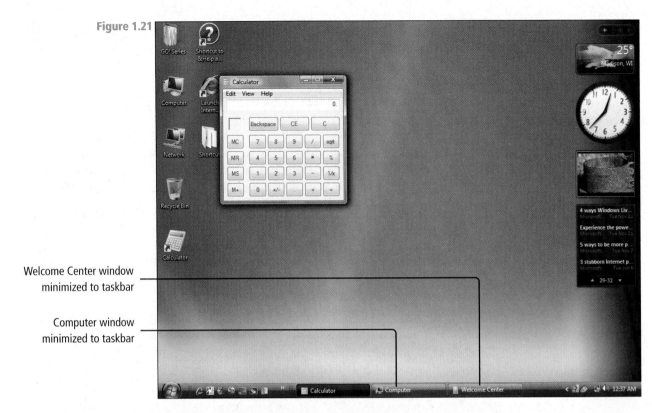

Welcome Center window
minimized to taskbar

Computer window
minimized to taskbar

5 In the taskbar, click the **Computer** button to restore the Computer window. Then, click the **Welcome Center** button to restore the Welcome Center window.

6 On the **Quick Launch** toolbar, click the **Show desktop** button [icon]. Compare your screen with Figure 1.22.

All open windows on the desktop are minimized, including the Windows Sidebar.

Figure 1.22

Show desktop button

Quick Launch toolbar

7 On the **Quick Launch** toolbar, click the **Show desktop** button again, and notice that all of the windows redisplay in their original locations. If you perform some action after you click the Show desktop button the first time, when you click it again, the windows will not redisplay—you will have to click the buttons for each window.

More Knowledge
Keeping More Than One Program Window Open at a Time

The ability to keep more than one window open at a time will become more useful as you become more familiar with Microsoft Office. For example, if you want to take information from two word processing documents to create a third document, you can open all three documents and use the taskbar to move among them, copying and pasting text from one document to another. Or, you could copy a chart from Excel and paste it into Word or take a table of data and paste it into PowerPoint. You can even have the same document open in two windows.

Objective 3
Resize, Move, and Scroll Windows

When a window opens on your screen, it generally opens in the same size and shape as it was when last used. If you are using more than one window at a time, you can increase or decrease the size of a window, or move a window so that you can see the information you need. As you work within a program, the information you create will likely grow larger than the screen can display. When the information in a window extends beyond the right or lower edges of the window, scroll bars display at the bottom and right. Using the *horizontal scroll bar*, you can move left and right to view information that extends beyond the left or right edge of the screen. Using the *vertical scroll bar*, you can move up and down to view information that extends beyond the top or bottom of the screen.

Activity 1.7 Previewing the Contents of the Taskbar

When you have a number of windows open, you may want to quickly review the contents of each document to determine which one to use.

1 On the taskbar, point to—but do not click—the **Computer** button, and then compare your screen with Figure 1.23.

A thumbnail of the window displays. A *thumbnail* is a miniature representation of a window or a file.

Figure 1.23

Thumbnail of the
Computer window

2 On the taskbar, point to—but do not click—the **Calculator** button.
Move the pointer and point to the **Welcome Center** button.

3 Click the **Start** button , click **All Programs**, click **Accessories**,
and then click **WordPad**. If the WordPad window is maximized, click

the Restore Down button .

WordPad is a simple word processing program that comes with
Vista, and generally opens maximized. Four programs are now open.

4 On the taskbar, click the **Switch between windows** button ,
and then compare your screen with Figure 1.24.

The screen displays a visual representation of the windows that are
open—called ***Flip 3D***—including the desktop. The taskbar buttons,
desktop icons, and Windows Sidebar gadget icons are all ***dimmed***—
displayed in a faded gray, which indicates that they are not currently
available.

Figure 1.24

Desktop

Calculator window

Computer window

Welcome Center window

WordPad window

Switch between windows button enables you to flip between open windows

5 On the keyboard, press ⬅, and notice that the last item in the list moves to the front.

6 Take a moment to press ⬅ and ➡ to scroll through the open windows.

7 Move the **Calculator** window to the front, and then press Enter. Alternatively, move the pointer to the desired window and click one time.

All of the windows display again, with the Calculator window on top.

8 Click anywhere on any of the windows behind the Calculator window, and notice that the window becomes the active window.

To make a window active, you can click on any part of the window that is visible. Recall that on the taskbar, the button for the active window is darker than the buttons for the other windows.

Activity 1.8 Cascading and Stacking Windows

In this activity, you will practice several other methods of displaying windows.

1 Click the **Start** button 🪟 , click **All Programs**, click **Accessories**, and then click **Paint**. If the Paint window opens maximized, click the Restore Down button 🗗 .

Paint is a program included with Vista in which graphics are created or edited.

2 On the taskbar, right-click anywhere in an open area—any area that is not on a button. From the displayed shortcut menu, click **Show Windows Stacked**, and then compare your screen with Figure 1.25.

The windows are ***stacked***—Vista reduces the size of the windows and tries to fit them all onto the screen at one time.

Figure 1.25

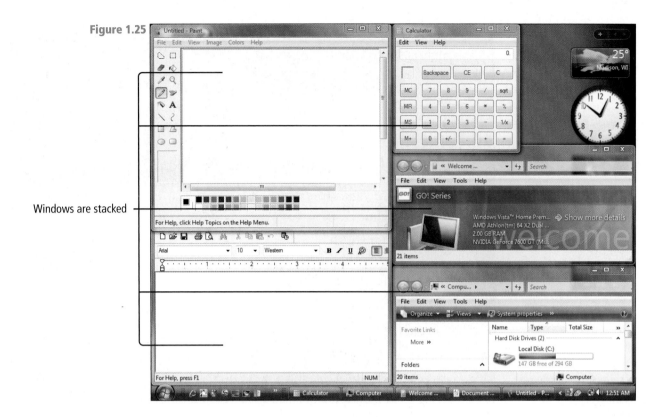

Windows are stacked

3 On the taskbar, right-click anywhere in an open area, and then from the shortcut menu, click **Undo Show Stacked**.

The windows return to their original shape, size, and location.

4 On the taskbar, right-click anywhere in an open area, and then from the shortcut menu, click **Cascade Windows**. Compare your screen with Figure 1.26.

When you **cascade** the open windows, they line up in a diagonal line from the upper left corner of the screen downward.

Figure 1.26

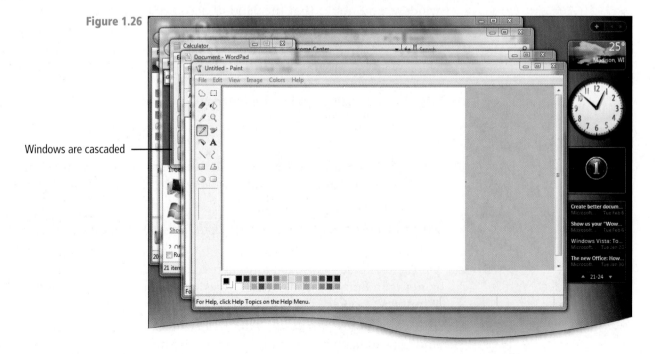

Windows are cascaded

5   On the taskbar, right-click anywhere in an open area, and then from the shortcut menu, click **Undo Cascade**.

Activity 1.9   Resizing, Moving, Scrolling, and Closing Windows

In the following activity, you will resize and move the Computer window. You will also use the vertical scroll bar in the Computer window to view information that does not fit in the window.

1   On the **Quick Launch** toolbar, click the **Show desktop** button .

2   On the taskbar, click the **Computer** button to display the Computer window.

3   Move the pointer to the lower right corner of the window to display the diagonal resize pointer , and then compare your screen with Figure 1.27.

    When the mouse pointer is in this shape, you can use it to change the size and shape of a window.

Figure 1.27

Diagonal resize pointer

4   Hold down the left mouse button, ***drag***—move the mouse while holding down the left mouse button, and then release at the appropriate time—diagonally up and to the left until you see a scroll bar at the right side of the window, and then release the mouse button. Adjust as necessary so that the Computer window is the approximate size of the one shown in Figure 1.28.

    Notice that a vertical scroll bar displays on the right side of the window. A scroll bar is added to the window whenever the window contains more than it can display.

Vertical scroll bar

Figure 1.28

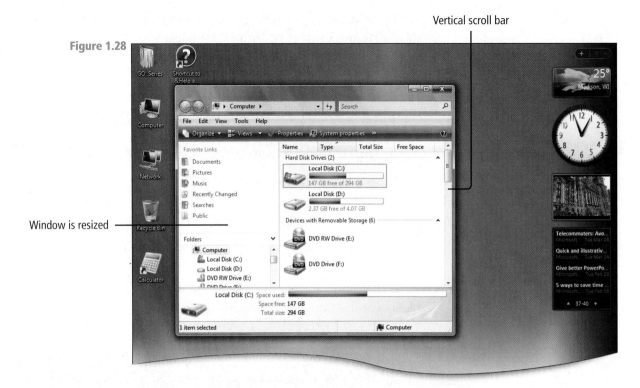

Window is resized

5 At the top of the **Computer** window, point to a blank area to the left of the Minimize, Maximize, and Close buttons. Hold down the left mouse button, drag—hold down the left mouse button, move the mouse, and then release the mouse button—up until the top edge of the window is just below the top of the screen.

6 In the Computer window, at the bottom of the vertical scroll bar, point to the **down arrow** ▼ and click four times. Notice that information at the bottom of the window scrolls up so that you can see the folders and icons that were not visible before, as shown in Figure 1.29.

Window moved to   Vertical scroll bar   Vertical scroll bar
the top of the screen   down arrow   up arrow

Figure 1.29

7 On the same scroll bar, point to the **up arrow**, and then click and hold down the left mouse button.

The list scrolls up to the top of the Content pane. You can click and hold down the left mouse button on the up or down scroll arrows to scroll rapidly through a long list of information.

8 Point to the scroll box, as shown in Figure 1.30, and then drag it downward.

The ***scroll box*** displays within the vertical and horizontal scroll bars and provides a visual indication of your location within the information displayed. It can also be used with the mouse to reposition the information on the screen. The size of the scroll box varies to indicate the relative size of the information. Moving the scroll box gives you more control as you scroll because you can see the information as it moves up or down in the window.

Vertical scroll box

Figure 1.30

Note — Moving a Screen at a Time

You can move up or down a screen at a time by clicking in the gray area above or below the vertical scroll box. You can also move left or right a screen at a time by clicking in the area to the left or right of a horizontal scroll box. The size of the scroll box indicates the relative size of the display to the whole document. If the scroll box is small, it means that the display is a small portion of the entire document.

9 On the taskbar, click the **Calculator** button to display the Calculator window.

The name of the window displays in the ***title bar***—a bar at the top of the window that displays the Minimize, Maximize, and Close buttons, the program icon, the window name, and sometimes the name of a saved document. Not all windows have all of these elements. Recall that the Computer window has the program icon and window name in the status bar, rather than in the title bar.

10 In the **Calculator** window, move the pointer to an open area of the title bar, and then drag the window to the approximate location shown in Figure 1.31.

Title bar

Figure 1.31

Program name

Program icon

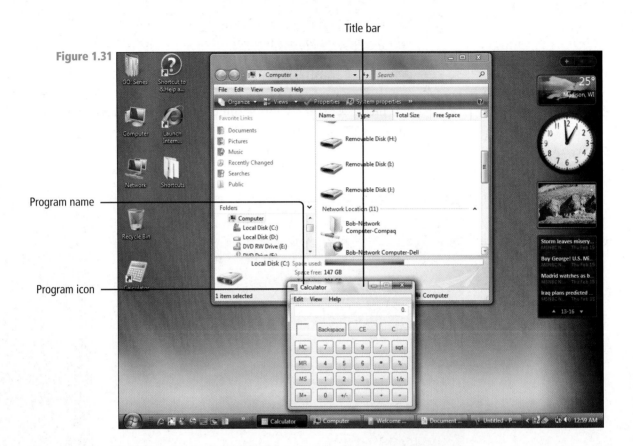

11 In the **Calculator** window title bar, click the **Close** button ![Close button].

The program closes, and the Calculator taskbar button is removed.

12 On the taskbar, right-click the **Welcome Center** button, and from the displayed shortcut menu, click **Close**.

Use a shortcut menu to close a program without having to view the program window.

13 Use either procedure you have practiced to close the remaining open windows.

End **You have completed Project 1A** _____

Project 1B Work with Files and Folders

In Activities 1.10 through 1.19 you will create folders, and then copy, move, rename, and delete files and folders. You will use the Vista search features to search for files, and you will use Vista Help to get information on how to use the operating system. Finally, you will capture a copy of your computer screen, open a word processing program, and paste the screen in the document, which will look similar to Figure 1.32.

For Project 1B, you will need the following files:

43 sample files, and two folders containing 14 additional files

You will save your document as
Captured_Screen_Firstname_Lastname

Figure 1.32
Project 1B—Work with Files and Folders

Objective 4
Create, Move, and Rename Folders

Information that you create in a computer program is stored in the computer's memory, which is a temporary storage location. This data may be lost if the computer is turned off. To keep the information you create, you must save it as a file on one of the drives available to you. For example, a five-page term paper that you create in a word processing program such as Microsoft Word, when saved, is a *file*. Files can be stored directly on a drive, but more commonly are stored in a folder on the drive. A *folder* is a container for programs and files, and is represented on the screen by a picture of a common paper file folder.

Use folders to organize the location of your programs and files so that you can easily locate them for later use. Folders and files must be created and stored on one of the drives attached to your computer. Your available drives fall into three categories: 1) the non-removable hard drive, also called the local disk, inside the computer; 2) removable drives that you insert into the computer, such as a flash drive, an external hard drive, or a writable CD or DVD; or 3) a shared network drive connected to your computer through a computer network, such as the network at your college.

Activity 1.10 Opening and Navigating Windows Explorer

Windows Explorer is a program that enables you to create and manage folders, and manage copy, move, sort, and delete files. In the following activity, you will create a folder on one of the three types of drives available to you—the local disk (hard drive), a removable drive (USB flash drive, an external hard drive, or some other type of removable drive), or a network drive. If you are using a computer in a college lab, you may have space assigned to you on a shared network drive. You can create these folders on any drive that is available to you. For the rest of this chapter, a USB drive will be used.

1 Click the **Start** button 🌐 , click **All Programs**, click **Accessories**, and then click **Windows Explorer**.

The Computer windows opens, with the Folders list on the Navigation pane displayed, and the Documents folder expanded.

2 On the toolbar, click the **Organize** button, and then point to **Layout**. If the Details pane does not display at the bottom of your window, click Details Pane. If the Navigation pane does not display on the left side of your window, repeat the procedure and click Navigation Pane. If the Folders list does not display, at the bottom of the Navigation pane, click Folders.

3 In the upper right corner of the **Windows Explorer** window, click the **Maximize** button ▣ to maximize the window, and then compare your screen with Figure 1.33. In the **Folders** list of the **Navigation** pane, use the vertical scroll bar to scroll up and down and examine the structure of the folders on your computer.

Figure 1.33

Organize button

Navigation pane

Folders list

Details pane

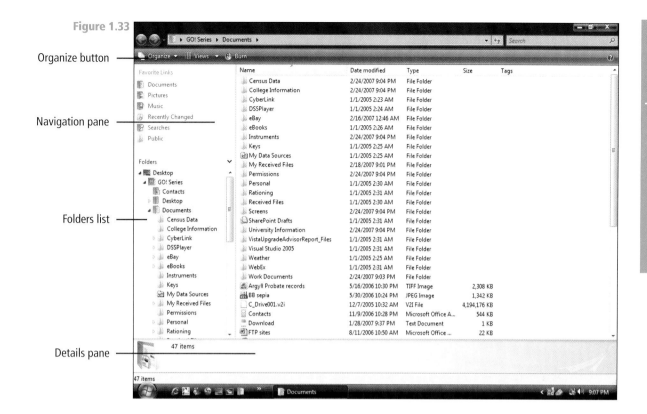

4 In the **Folders** list, scroll down, and then click **Computer**.

The Content pane displays a list of hard drives, removable storage devices, available network locations, and other devices connected to the computer.

5 In the **Folders** list, to the left of **Computer**, click the open triangle ▷. Notice that the triangle changes to a filled triangle pointing downward at an angle ◢.

The open triangle indicates that there are other folders and drives to be displayed. When you click the open triangle, the next level of folders and drives displays.

6 Insert your USB flash drive or other removable drive. If an action dialog box displays asking what you want Windows to do, click **Cancel**. Scroll down in the **Folders** list, and then click your removable drive—for this chapter, the removable drive name will be LEXAR MEDIA (K:). Compare your screen with Figure 1.34. Notice that the Content pane in the figure is empty; your storage device or drive may already contain files and folders.

Figure 1.34

Content pane is empty

Flash drive

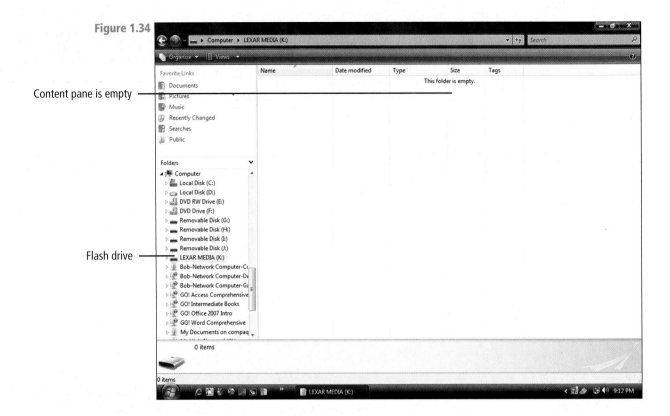

More Knowledge

Computer Storage Devices

The hard drive (local disk) is usually identified on your computer by the notation C:\ (and sometimes D:\, E:\, and so on for additional drives). *Flash drives*—also known as *USB drives* or *thumb drives*—are small storage devices that plug into a computer Universal Serial Bus (USB) port, a connection between a computer and a peripheral device such as a printer, a mouse, a keyboard, or a USB drive.

You may also have access to files on another type of storage device, a *CD*— Compact Disc, or a *DVD*—Digital Video (or Versatile) Disc. CD and DVD drives are optical storage devices that come in two formats—read-only and read-write. If you are using files stored on a read-only CD or a DVD disc, you will need to open a file from the disc, and then save it to a writable drive, or copy a file to another disk and then open it.

Activity 1.11 Creating a New Folder

It is always a good idea to create a new folder when you have a new category of files to store. You do not need to create a new folder for each type of file, however. You can store many different kinds of files in the same folder.

1 With the removable drive selected, in an open area of the **Content** pane, right-click to display a shortcut menu, and then point to **New**. Compare your screen with Figure 1.35.

Figure 1.35

Create a new folder here

Shortcut menu

New command

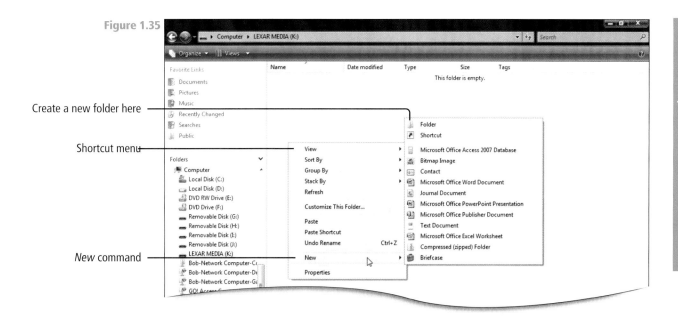

2 From the shortcut menu, click **Folder**.

A new folder—named *New Folder*—is created with the name of the folder displayed in the *edit mode*. Edit mode enables you to change the name of a file or folder, and works the same in all Windows programs.

3 With *New Folder* selected, substitute your name where indicated, and type **Word Documents of Firstname Lastname** and then press Enter. Click anywhere in the blank area of the Content pane to deselect the new folder and compare your screen with Figure 1.36.

Figure 1.36

Renamed folder

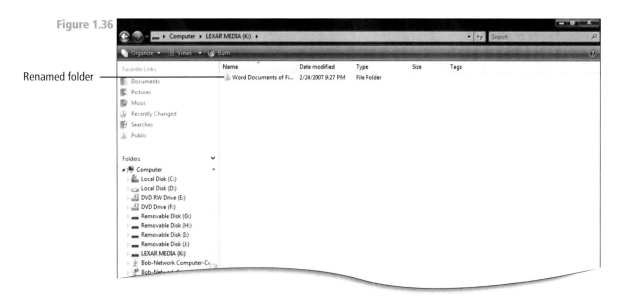

Another Way — **To Rename a Folder**

If you accidentally press Enter before you have a chance to name the folder, you can still rename it. Right-click the folder, click Rename from the shortcut menu, type a new name, and then press Enter. Alternatively, you can click the folder once, pause, and then click the folder again to activate edit mode.

4 With the removable drive still selected, in an open area of the **Content** pane, right-click to display a shortcut menu, point to **New**, and then click **Folder**. Type **Pictures of Firstname Lastname** and then press [Enter].

Two new folders have been created in your storage location. Notice the order in which the folders display.

5 In the **Content** pane, click the **Name** column heading several times to sort the folders and file names from a to z and from z to a. Notice that the arrow in the Name column heading points up when the folders are displayed in *ascending order* (*a* to *z*), and points down when the folders are displayed in *descending order* (*z* to *a*). Stop when the folders are sorted in descending alphabetical order—from z to a.

6 In the **Content** pane, move the pointer to the line at the right of the **Name** column heading to display the resize pointer ⊞, as shown in Figure 1.37. Drag the resize pointer to the right to make the column slightly wider than the longest folder name.

Name column heading with
arrow indicating sort order

Figure 1.37

Files in descending
alphabetical order

Resize pointer

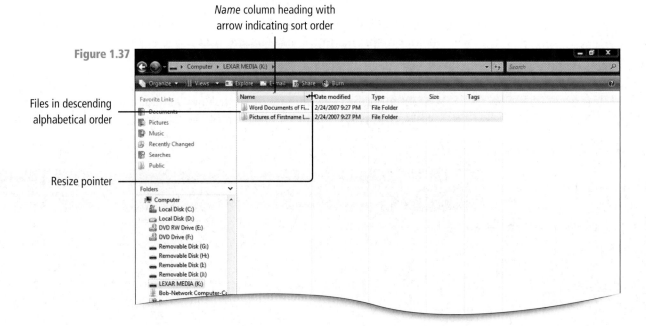

Activity 1.12 Moving and Renaming Folders

Your student files and folders are stored on a CD or another location chosen by your instructor. You can move the folders, including the files in the folders, from another location to your flash drive or other storage device.

1 Navigate to the location where your student files for this book are stored. They may be stored on a CD, in a course management system, on a hard drive, or on a shared network drive.

2 Locate and click the folder named **chapter_01_windows_vista**, and then compare your screen with Figure 1.38. If your files and folders do not display the way they display in the figure, on the toolbar, click the Views button, and then click Details.

There are two folders and a number of files in this folder. The total number of files and folders is displayed in the Details pane at the bottom of the screen. There are more files in the two folders, but they are not included in the totals in the Details pane—only the files and the folders currently displayed in the Content pane are counted.

Files

Figure 1.38

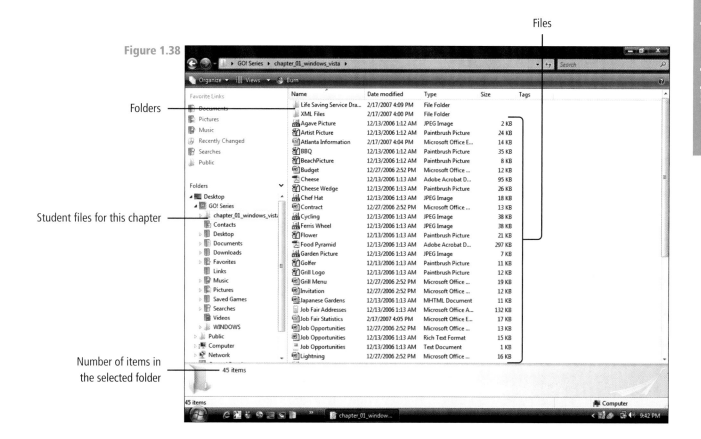

Folders

Student files for this chapter

Number of items in the selected folder

3 In the **Content** pane, move the pointer to the right border of the **Name** column heading to display the ⊞ pointer. Double-click to resize the border to the widest folder or file name. Repeat this procedure to display the full **Date modified** and **Type** column contents.

Note — Changing the Columns that Display in the Content Pane

If one or more of the columns displayed in Figure 1.38 do not display, right-click anywhere in the Content pane column titles, and then check the desired column.

4 In the **Folders** list, scroll as necessary to display your flash drive or other storage device. Be sure your student files and folders still display in the Content pane.

5 Locate the **XML Files** folder near the top of the **Content** pane. Click on the folder, hold the mouse button down, and drag the folder to the **Folders** list directly on top of your storage drive, as shown in

Figure 1.39. Notice that a folder displays attached to the pointer, and a ScreenTip says *Copy to LEXAR MEDIA (K:)*—your folder or drive name will vary.

Figure 1.39

ScreenTip indicates
copy location

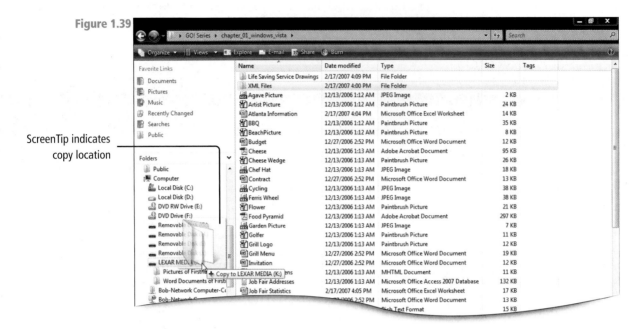

☐6 Release the mouse button.

☐7 Repeat the procedure you just practiced to copy the **Life Saving Service Drawings** folder to your storage area, and notice that a message box indicates the progress of the copy.

The message box displays because the size of the *Life Saving Service Drawings* folder is much larger than the size of the *XML Files* folder.

Figure 1.40

Message box indicates
progress of the copy

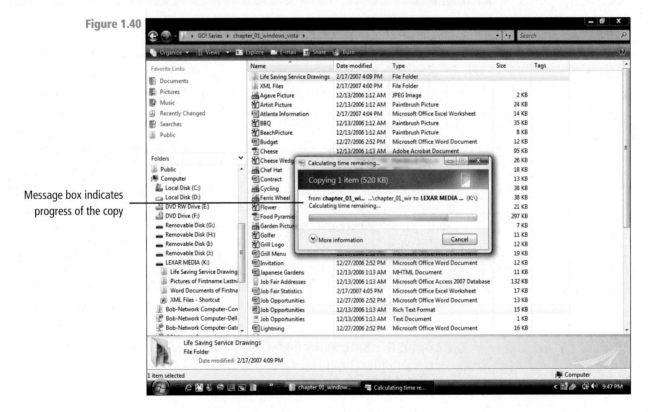

8 In the **Folders** list, click the flash drive or other device where you are storing your files and folders. In the **Content** pane, right-click the **Life Saving Service Drawings** folder, and then from the displayed shortcut menu, click **Rename**.

9 With the folder name in edit mode, type **LSS Drawings** and then press [Enter].

The folder name is changed. When text is selected, typing replaces all of the selected text.

Objective 5
Copy, Move, Rename, and Delete Files

Recall that Windows manages your data files because your files are stored on the drives attached to your computer. Copying files from one folder to another is a frequent data management task. For example, you might want to make a backup copy of important information, copy a file from a CD to a local disk, or copy information from your local disk drive to a removable drive. Copying files works the same regardless of the type of drive.

Performing other operations on files, such as deleting them or moving them, also works the same regardless of the type of drive. As you accumulate files, you will likely need to delete some to reduce clutter on your hard drive. You might also want to move documents into other folders on another drive to *archive* them—place them somewhere for long-term storage. Finally, you may want to change the names of file to make the names more descriptive. All of these tasks are functions of your Windows Vista operating system.

Activity 1.13 Copying Files

1 In the **Folders** list, scroll to the location where your student files for this book are stored. Locate and click the folder named **chapter_01_windows_vista** to display the files and folders in the folder.

2 In the **Folders** list, scroll as necessary to display your flash drive or other storage device. Be sure your student files and folders still display in the Content pane.

3 Near the top of the **Content** pane, locate the **BeachPicture** file, and then drag it to your storage device. Recall that dragging also includes releasing the mouse button at the destination location.

When you drag a file or folder from one device to another, it is copied, which means that the original file remains on the original drive, and a copy of the file is placed on the new drive. If you drag a file or folder to another place (such as a folder) on the *same* drive—for example, from one folder to another—the file or folder is moved and no longer resides in the original location.

4 Use the same procedure to move the **Budget** file to your storage device, and then in the **Folders** list, click your storage device. Click the **Name** column heading as necessary to sort the folder in ascending order—the arrow should be pointing up. Compare your screen with Figure 1.41.

The Content pane should display four folders—the two that you created, and the two that you copied. In addition, the two files that you copied should display below the folders. When you sort a folder in ascending order, the folders always display first.

Folders display first

Figure 1.41

Folders and files sorted in alphabetical order by Name

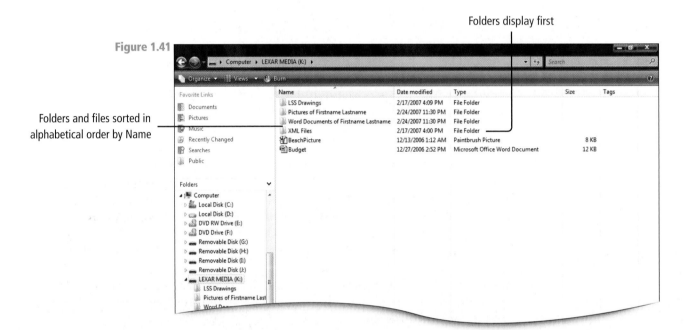

5 Display the files and folders in the **chapter_01_windows_vista** folder again. Click the **Agave Picture** file, hold down ⇧Shift, and then click the **BBQ** file.

By holding down the Shift key, you select the two files you click and all of the files in between.

6 In the **Folders** list, scroll as necessary to display your storage area. Drag the selected files to your storage area.

7 Click the **Chef Hat** file, hold down Ctrl, and then click the **Food Pyramid** file, and then the **Grill Logo** file. Notice that by using the Control key, you can select several files that are not next to each other, as shown in Figure 1.42.

Figure 1.42

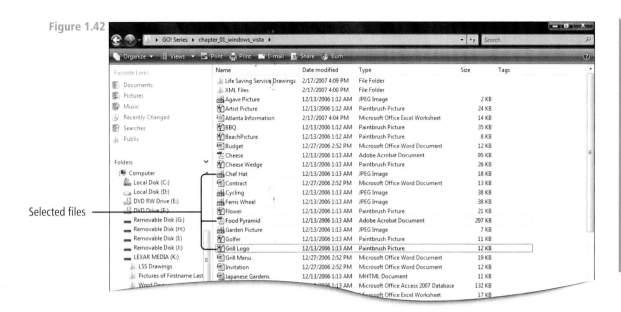

Selected files

8 Drag the selected files to your storage area.

9 In the **Content** pane, click the **Grill Menu** file, and then use the vertical scroll bar to scroll to the bottom of the pane. Hold down ⟨⇧Shift⟩, and then click the **Waterride** file. In the Detail area, notice that the number of files and the total size of the selected files displays, as shown in Figure 1.43.

Selected files

Figure 1.43

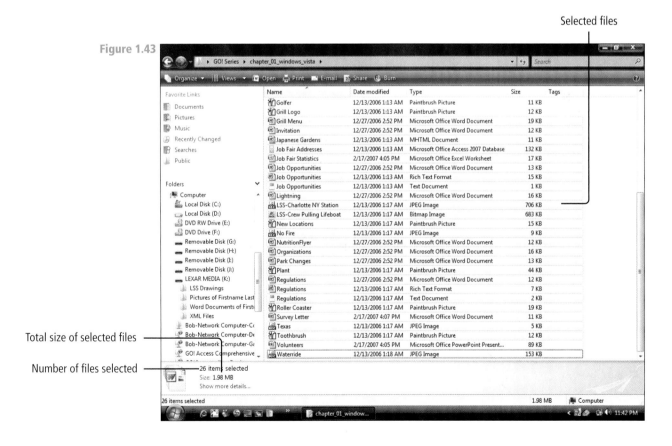

Total size of selected files

Number of files selected

10 Drag the selected files to your storage area.

More Knowledge
File Extensions

The files you see may display three or four letters following the file name, such as .docx. These are *file extensions*, and most files have these extensions—although they may or may not display on your system. Files created by Microsoft Office programs have a standard set of extensions that identify the type of program used to create the file. For example, Microsoft Word documents end in .doc or .docx, Excel worksheets end in .xls or .xlsx, PowerPoint presentations end with .ppt or pptx, and so on.

Activity 1.14 Moving, Renaming, and Deleting Files

In the following activity, you will move files from one location on your removable drive to another location on the same drive. You will also rename and delete files.

1 In the **Folders** list, scroll as necessary and then click on your flash drive or other storage device.

Your storage device should display four folders at the top, and a total of 39 items in the folder, as displayed in the Details pane.

2 In the **Content** pane, click the **Type** column header to sort the files by file type. Move the pointer to the right border of the **Type** column heading to display the ⊹ pointer. Double-click to resize the border to the widest file type—*Microsoft Office PowerPoint Presentation*.

3 In the **Content** pane, use the wheel in the middle of your mouse to scroll down until you can see all of the *Microsoft Office Word Document* files. If you do not have a mouse wheel, use the vertical scroll bar.

4 Click the **Budget** file, hold down ⇧ Shift, and then click the **Survey Letter** file to select all of the Word documents. Drag the selected files to the **Word Documents of Firstname Lastname** folder.

The files are moved to the new folder, and no longer display in their original location.

5 In the **Folders** list, click the **Word Documents of Firstname Lastname** folder, and then compare your screen with Figure 1.44.

Figure 1.44

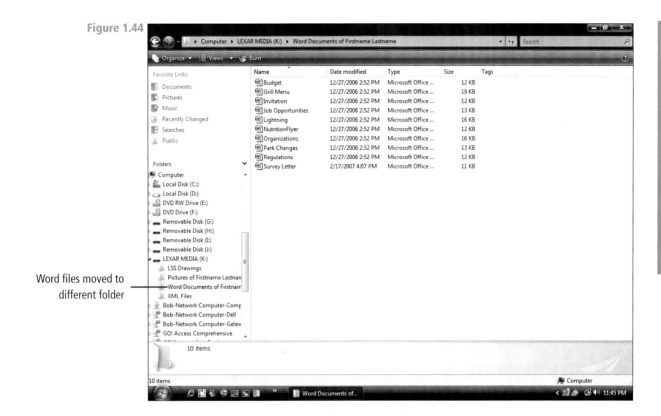

Word files moved to
different folder

In the **Folders** list, click on your flash drive or other storage device. Using the technique you just practiced, select the six **JPEG Images**, and then drag them to the **Pictures of Firstname Lastname** folder.

Select the **LSS-Crew Pulling Lifeboat** file and drag it to the **Pictures of Firstname Lastname** folder. Then, select all eight **Paintbrush Picture** files and drag them to the **Pictures of Firstname Lastname** folder.

Alert!

What if Paintbrush Picture file types do not display?

Paintbrush Picture file types may also be called something different, depending on the way files are associated with programs on your computer. These files are Windows Metafile images, and have a *.wmf* extension. There will be eight pictures with the same type displayed, including *Artist Picture*, *BBQ*, and so forth. If your file types differ, use these eight files in place of the Paintbrush Picture files.

In the **Folders** list, click the **Pictures of Firstname Lastname** folder, and then compare your screen with Figure 1.45.

Figure 1.45

Three kinds of picture files
moved to new folder

9 On the toolbar, click the **Views** button, and then click **Large Icons**.

Thumbnail images display for recognized file types, while the other files display a placeholder image.

10 In the **Content** pane, right-click the **Agave Picture** file, and then click **Rename**. Type **Agave Cactus** and then press Enter.

11 In the **Content** pane, right-click the **No Fire** file, and then click **Delete**. The **Delete File** message box displays, as shown in Figure 1.46.

Figure 1.46

Delete File message box
asks for confirmation of delete

12 In the **Delete File** message box, click **Yes** to send the file to the Recycle Bin.

13 In the upper left corner of the **Windows Explorer** window, click the **Back** button 🔙 to move back to your main storage area. Alternatively, in the Folders list, click your storage location name.

14 In the **Content** pane, right-click the **XML Files** folder, and then click **Delete**. In the displayed **Delete Folder** message box, click **Yes**.

When you delete a folder, all files in the folder are also deleted.

Activity 1.15 Compressing Files

Some files may be too large to send quickly as an e-mail attachment. For example, files containing graphics tend to be quite large. Windows Vista includes a feature with which you can **compress**—reduce the file size of—one or more files into a single file that uses a *.zip* file extension. These files can then be uncompressed for editing on any other computer running Windows Vista. Many file types—such as Microsoft Office 2007 files, Adobe Acrobat files, and JPEG picture files—do not benefit much from file compression. However, compression is often used to combine many files into one file for easy distribution.

1 With your storage device selected, and three folders and ten files displayed in the **Content** pane, click the **Food Pyramid** file, hold down Shift, and then click the second **Regulations** file. If your files are in a different order, select all ten files, but not the folders. Notice that the Details pane indicates that ten files are selected, with a total size of 582 KB.

2 In the **Content** pane, right-click any of the selected files, and then from the displayed shortcut menu, point to **Send To**. Compare your screen with Figure 1.47.

Figure 1.47

Compressed (zipped) Folder command

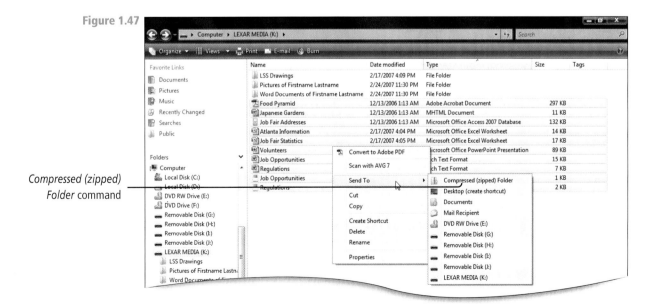

3 From the displayed list, click **Compressed (zipped) Folder**.

The compressed folder displays the name of the file you right-clicked, but displays in edit mode so you can change the file name.

Note — To Work with Third-Party Zip Programs

If you are using a third-party zip program, such as WinZip™ or PKZIP™, you will need to use that program to complete this task—the procedure listed below may not work.

---

4 With the compressed folder name still in edit mode, type **Files of Firstname Lastname** and then press Enter. Notice that the compressed folder size is now just under 400 KB, or about two-thirds the size of the ten selected files. Compare your screen with Figure 1.48.

Compressed folder

Figure 1.48

File size reduced by about one-third

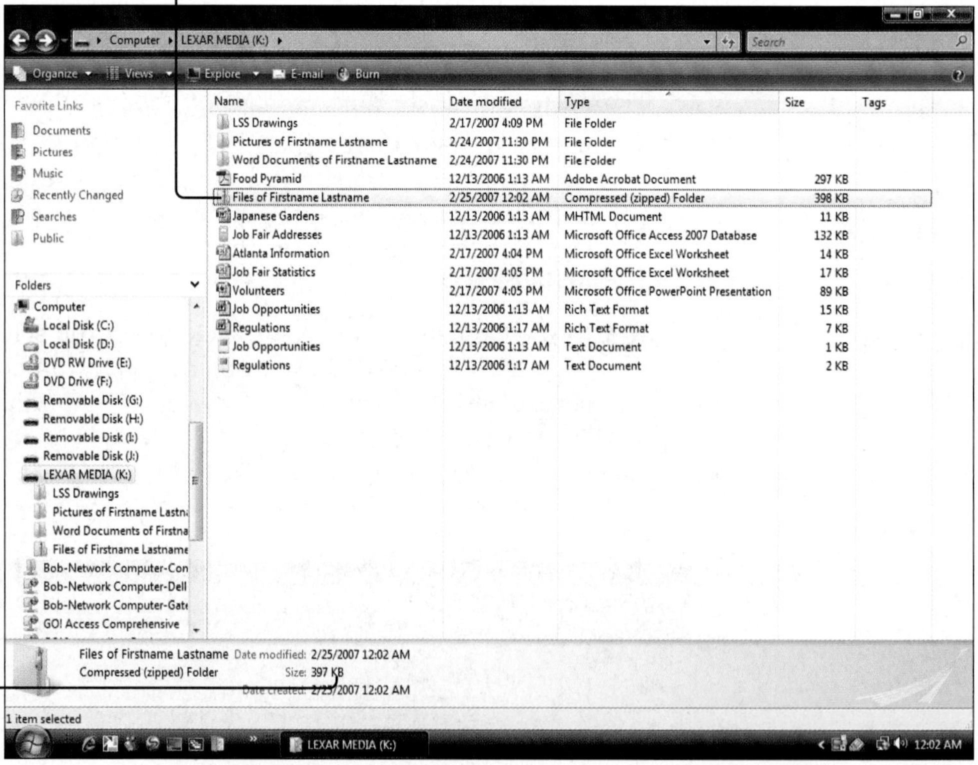

5 In the **Content** pane, double-click the **Files of Firstname Lastname** compressed folder. Compare your screen with Figure 1.49.

The files in the compressed folder are listed, along with their original sizes and their compressed sizes. The percent of space saved is indicated for each file. Some of the files show very little space savings, while in others the space saved is considerable. To extract the files from the compressed folder, click the *Extract all files* button on the toolbar. You can also open the files directly from the compressed folder.

Figure 1.49

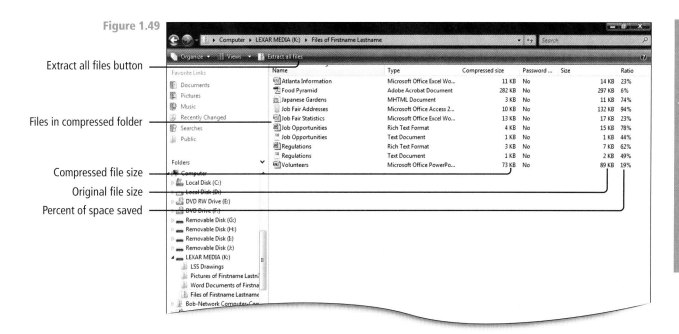

Extract all files button

Files in compressed folder

Compressed file size
Original file size
Percent of space saved

More Knowledge

Adding More Items to a Compressed Folder

You can add more files to an existing compressed folder by dragging files and dropping them on the compressed folder. You can drag the files to the folder from anywhere, and you can also drag folders into a compressed folder.

Activity 1.16 Capturing an Image of a Screen

Windows includes a screen capture utility so that you can capture an image of your screen and then print it or save it as a file. This can come in handy if you want to save something you found on a Web site, or if you need to document a screen problem or an error message.

1 In the upper left corner of the window, click the **Back** button ![Back button] to move back to your main storage area. Alternatively, in the Folders list, click your storage location name. Be sure that three folders, one compressed folder, and ten files are displayed in the **Content** pane. If necessary, Maximize ![Maximize button] the Computer window.

2 On your keyboard, locate and press PrtScr.

The Print Screen key on your keyboard is commonly located near the right side of the top row of keys. This key captures an image of the entire screen and places it in a temporary storage area called the **Clipboard**. Items in the Clipboard can be placed in a document using the Paste command.

3 Click the **Start** button ![Start button], click **All Programs**, and then locate and click **Microsoft Office Word 2007**. If necessary, Maximize ![Maximize button] the Word window.

If you do not have Microsoft Word available, open any other word processing program.

4 In the **Word** window, using your own name, type **Firstname Lastname** and then press Enter.

5 Near the top left corner of the screen, click the **Paste** button. Use the vertical scroll bar to move to the top of the document, and then compare your screen with Figure 1.50.

The captured screen that has been stored in your Clipboard is pasted at the insertion point.

Figure 1.50

Paste button

Captured screen

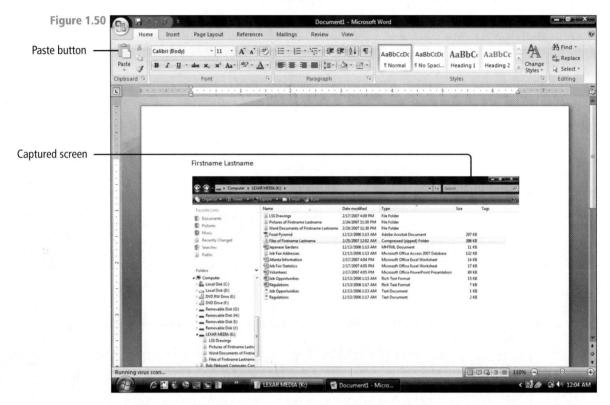

6 At the upper left corner of the Word window, click the **Office** button , and then click **Save As**. In the **Save As** dialog box, in the **Navigation** pane, click **Computer**. Locate and click your storage device. If you are using another storage area, click Documents and navigate to the location of your stored files.

7 Near the bottom of the **Save As** dialog box, in the **File Name** box, type **Captured Screen Firstname Lastname** and then at the bottom of the dialog box, click **Save**.

8 Check your *Course Syllabus* or *Chapter Assignment Sheet*, or ask your instructor, to determine if you are to submit a printed or electronic copy of this file. To print, click the **Office** button , point to **Print**, and then click **Quick Print**. To submit electronically, using your college's course management system, consult your instructor's directions for saving and submitting the file.

9 Click the **Office** button , and then at the bottom right corner of the displayed list, click **Exit Word**.

Objective 6
Find Files and Folders

As you use a computer, you will likely accumulate a large number of files and folders. It's easy to forget where you stored a file, or what you named it. Windows Vista provides several search functions with which you can find files and folders. You can also add tags to files. *Tags* are custom file properties that help you find and organize your files. Tags are part of a file's *metadata*—items that record and display information about a file, such as a title, a rating, the file name, and the file size.

Activity 1.17 Adding Descriptions and Tags to Files

1 Be sure your storage device is selected, and three folders, one compressed folder, and eleven files are displayed in the **Content** pane. Also be sure the Details pane is open at the bottom of the window. If necessary, Maximize the Computer window. If your files display as a list, on the toolbar, click the Views button, and then click Large Icons.

2 In the **Navigation** pane, in the **Folders** list, click the **LSS Drawings** folder, and then click the file **LSS-Dragging Surfboat to Beach**.

3 In the **Details** pane, click in the **Tags** box—to the right of the word *Tags*. Type **LSS** and then press →. Type **LSS Boat** and then press →. Type **Surfboat** and then compare your screen with Figure 1.51. Notice on the left side of the Details pane that the file type for this file is JPEG—one of a number of image file types. If a pop-up box displays, ignore it.

When you add a tag, a semicolon immediately displays to the right of the insertion point. Semicolons separate multiple tags.

Figure 1.51

Selected file

Semicolons separate tags

New tags added

4 Press [Enter] to confirm the tags. Using the procedure you just practiced, add the same three tags to the **LSS-Surf Boat in High Surf** file. Notice on the left side of the Details pane that the file type for this file is JPEG.

5 Click the **LSS-Self-Righting Lifeboat with Sail** file. Notice that there is no place to add a tag.

This image is a bitmap image, which doesn't support tags. All Microsoft Office 2007 default file formats support tags, as do many other types of programs.

6 In the **Navigation** pane, in the **Folders** list, click the **Pictures of Firstname Lastname** folder, and then click the file **LSS-Charlotte NY Station**. Add the following tags: **LSS** and **LSS Boat** and **LSS Boat Ramp** and then press [Enter].

7 In the **Details** pane, click the **Title** box, type **Life Saving Station at Charlotte, NY** and then press [Enter].

8 In the **Content** pane, right click the **LSS-Charlotte NY Station** file, and then from the shortcut menu, click **Properties**. In the **Properties** dialog box, click the **Details tab**.

The items you entered in the Details pane display, and there are several other categories of tags that you can add, including a rating of the picture or document.

9 In the **Properties** dialog box, under **Description**, click the fourth **Rating** star from the left. Under **Origin**, click the **Copyright** box, type **Public Domain** and then compare your screen with Figure 1.52.

Selected file

Figure 1.52

Title added
Rating tag
New tags added

Copyright information

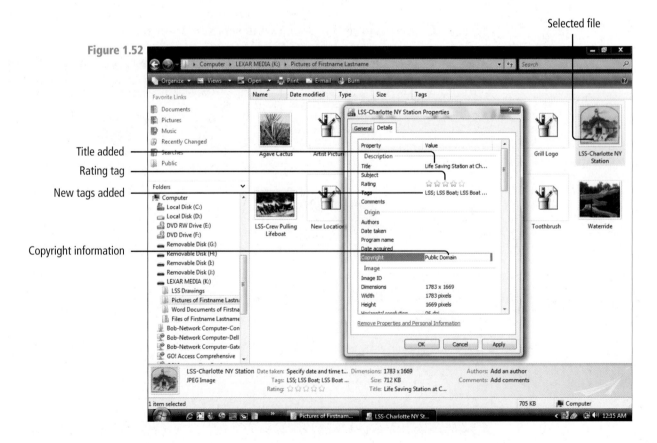

10 At the bottom of the **Properties** dialog box, click **OK** to close the dialog box.

Activity 1.18 Finding Files and Folders and Creating a Search Folder

1 In the **Folders** list, click your storage location name. Be sure your storage device is selected, and three folders, one compressed folder, and eleven files display in the **Content** pane.

2 Near the upper right corner of the window, click in the **Search** box, type **J** and then in the **Content** pane, examine the results of your search, as shown in Figure 1.53.

The program found all files and folders that contain the letter *J*, along with all file types that contain the letter *J*—in this case, all JPEG image files. A *Search Results* folder displays in the Folders list.

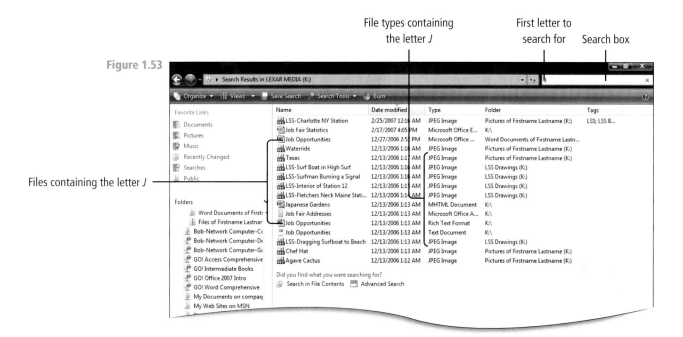

Figure 1.53

3 Type the letter **P** and examine the search results. Notice that the only files, folders, or file types in your storage device that contain the consecutive letters *JP* are the JPEG image files.

4 Press ⟨← Bksp⟩, and notice that the search results again display all files, folders, and file types that contain the letter *J*.

5 Now type **ob** to complete the word *Job*. Notice that five files display, as shown in Figure 1.54.

Search term

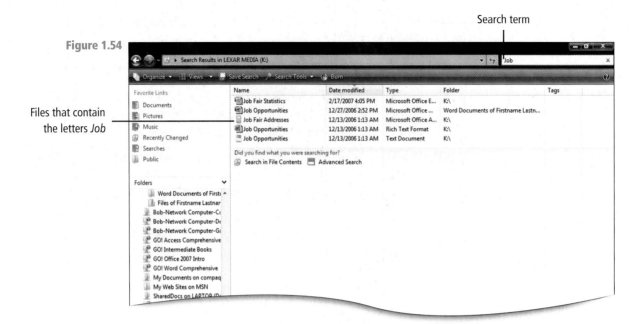

Figure 1.54

Files that contain the letters *Job*

---

6 Press ◄─Bksp three times, type **LSS** and then notice that files and folders from various locations display in the Content pane.

7 Press Spacebar, type **boat** and then notice that only one file or folder meets this search condition, even though you added *LSS Boat* as a tag to several files. Also notice that the file that was found had both search words, but they do not have to be next to each other.

When you enter a word or phrase in the Search box, only the file names, folder names, and file types are searched.

8 In the **Navigation** pane, in the **Folders** list, right-click your storage device, and then from the shortcut menu, click **Search**. On the right side of the menu bar, click the **Advanced Search arrow**.

The Advanced Search enables you to search for tags, authors, or names. It also enables you to search for the date the file was created or last saved.

Note — Searching Document Contents

If you conduct a search from the Search box and do not find what you need, you can also search for documents that contain key words or phrases *in the document*. To search for document contents, in the Content pane, at the bottom of the search results, click Search in File Contents.

---

9 In the **Tags** box, type **LSS Boat** and then click the **Search** button. Notice that all of the files with LSS Boat tags display in the search results, as shown in Figure 1.55.

Figure 1.55

Search term in *Tags* box

Save Search button

Files that include *LSS Boat* tag

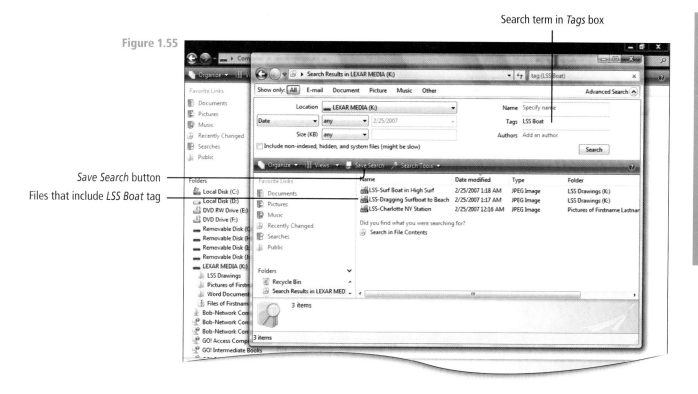

10 On the toolbar, click the **Save Search** button. In the displayed **Save As** dialog box, click **Save**.

A **search folder** is saved on your computer—not on your removable storage device. A search folder retains all of the search conditions you specified during your search, and re-creates the search every time you click the search folder. As you add more pictures with the *LSS Boat* tag to your removable storage device, the search folder will find them. It is important to remember that the search folder will only search the location you specified—it will not search the rest of the computer.

11 **Close** the Search Results dialog box.

12 In the **Navigation** pane, in the **Folders** list, scroll up and locate the **Searches** folder. Click the open triangle to the left of **Searches**, and then notice that your search is saved there, as shown in Figure 1.56.

Figure 1.56

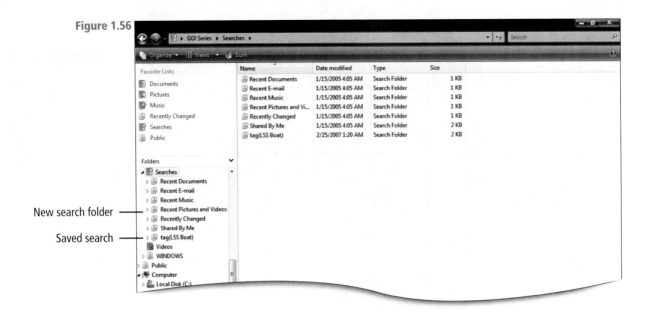

New search folder

Saved search

More Knowledge

Using Wildcards in Searches

When you are searching for a particular type of file, you can specify the extension by using a wildcard, followed by the extension. A *wildcard* takes the place of one or more characters in a search. For example, if you wanted to search for all of your Excel 2007 files in the Document folder, select the folder, and then type *.xlsx* in the Search box. All files with the .xlsx extension will display. If you want to display all your Excel files, including older versions (with the .xls extension), type *.xls*. This search will locate all .xls and .xlsx files. Similarly, you can search for all files beginning with *Fun* by typing *Fun**, which will return all files with those first three letters, including *Fundamentals of Business* and *Fun with Trombones*.

Objective 7
Use Vista Help

There will be times that you can't figure out how to make Vista do what you want it to do. Microsoft offers a robust Help system that enables you to read instructions on topics of your choice, and in some cases even walks you through the steps to accomplish a task. Help is available both installed on your computer and online.

Activity 1.19 Using Vista Help

1 With **Windows Explorer** open, on the right side of the toolbar, click the **Get help** button 🔘.

The Windows Help and Support dialog box displays, with some general topics of interest, a Search box, and a link to Online Help.

2 In the displayed **Windows Help and Support** dialog box, in the **Search** box, type **Quick Launch toolbar** and then press Enter. Compare your screen with Figure 1.57.

Several topics associated with the Quick Launch toolbar display.

Figure 1.57

Search term

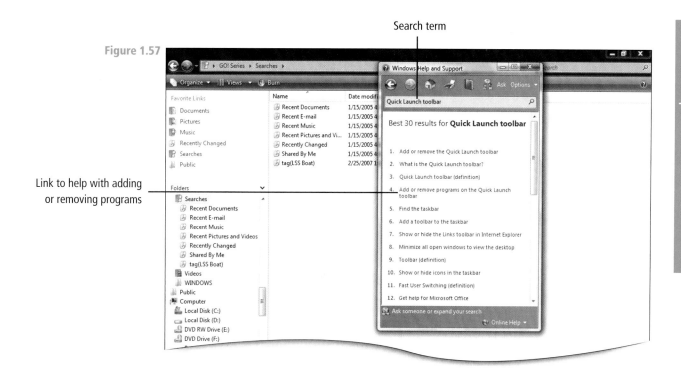

Link to help with adding or removing programs

3 In the list of associated topics, click **Add or remove programs on the Quick Launch toolbar**, and notice the help that is available.

The green text indicates links to definitions; the blue text indicates that the text can be expanded to display more information.

4 In the **Windows Help and Support** dialog box, click the blue text **To add a program icon to the Quick Launch toolbar** to expand the topic. In the paragraph below the topic title, click the green text *Quick Launch toolbar*, and then compare your screen with Figure 1.58.

Figure 1.58

Green text indicates a definition

Definition of *Quick Launch toolbar*

Blue text indicates further information

Expanded topic

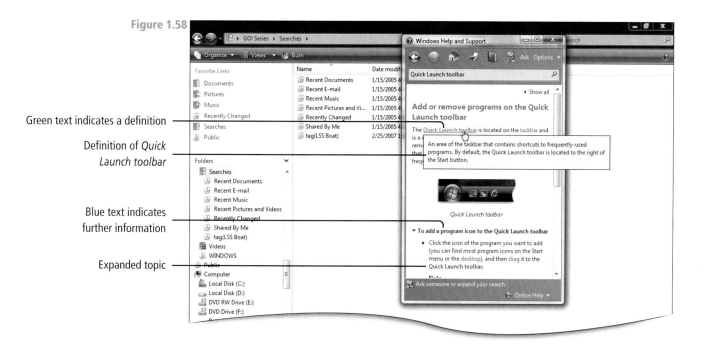

5 In the **Search** box, select and delete the existing text, type **Show file extensions** and then press Enter. From the displayed list, click **Show or hide file name extensions**, and then compare your screen with Figure 1.59.

There are three ways to get help on this topic. If you scroll down the dialog box, you will see the steps involved in showing—or hiding—file extensions. Near the top of the dialog box are two other options. One walks you through the steps automatically, while you watch. The second—*guided help*—stops at each step, and you actually perform the steps.

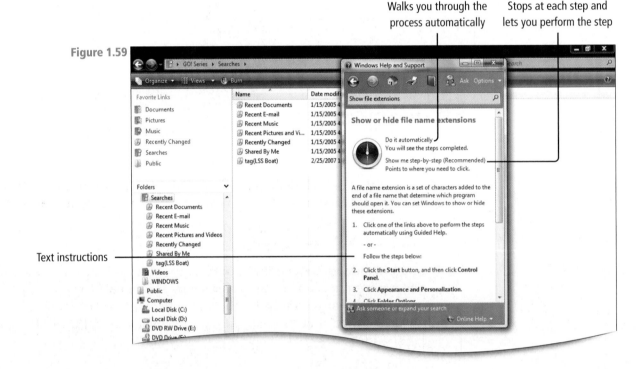

Walks you through the
process automatically

Stops at each step and
lets you perform the step

Figure 1.59

Text instructions

6 Click **Show me step-by-step (Recommended)**. In the first **Guided Help** dialog box, notice that the first step is to click the Start button, and that everything else on the screen is gray except the correct location.

7 Click the **Start** button to move to the next **Guided Help** dialog box. Continue moving through the process until the **Folder Options** dialog box displays, as shown in Figure 1.60.

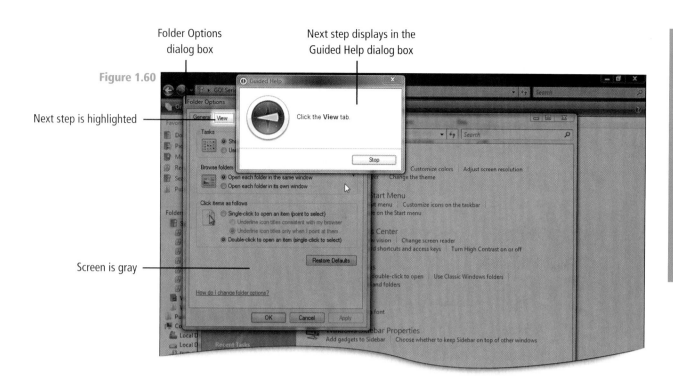

Figure 1.60

Folder Options dialog box

Next step is highlighted

Screen is gray

Next step displays in the Guided Help dialog box

8 Unless you want to turn the file extensions on or off, in the **Guided Help** dialog box, click **Stop**, and then click **Exit**. **Close** all remaining dialog boxes and windows.

More Knowledge
Printing Help

If you wish to print the help topic for future reference, on the toolbar, click the Print button, or click the Options button, and then click Print.

End **You have completed Project 1B**

Content-Based Assessments

Summary

Windows Vista is a robust operating system that enables you to easily locate information and programs. It enables you to create, rename, move, copy, and delete files and folders. You can add key words and other information to the files to make searching easier and more accurate.

Key Terms

Content-Based Assessments

Match each term in the second column with its correct definition in the first column. Write the letter of the term on the blank line in front of the correct definition.

_____ **1.** The Vista user interface that features a three-dimensional look, with transparent window frames, live previews of open windows, and multiple color schemes.

_____ **2.** The pane on the left side of the Computer or Windows Explorer window that contains Personal folders and the Folders list.

_____ **3.** Displays information about the drive, folder, or file selected in the Content pane.

_____ **4.** A set of instructions that coordinates the activities of your computer.

_____ **5.** A computer interface that shows documents as they will look in their final form and uses icons to represent programs.

_____ **6.** Part of the Navigation pane that displays the drive and folder structure on the computer.

_____ **7.** Displays the Start button and the name of any open documents; it may also display shortcut buttons for other programs.

_____ **8.** Command at the bottom of the Start menu that takes you to all available programs on your computer.

_____ **9.** To remove the window from the screen without closing it.

_____ **10.** To increase the size of a window to fill the screen.

_____ **11.** The bar at the right side of a window that enables you to move up and down to view information that extends beyond the top and bottom of the screen.

_____ **12.** The bar at the bottom of a window that enables you to move left and right to view information that extends beyond the left and right edges of the screen.

_____ **13.** Move the mouse pointer while holding down the left mouse button, and then release at the appropriate time.

_____ **14.** Work that you save and store on a drive, such as a Word document or a PowerPoint presentation.

_____ **15.** A program that enables you to create and manage folders, and manage copy, move, sort, and delete files.

A All Programs

B Details pane

C Drag

D File

E Folders list

F Graphical user interface

G Horizontal scroll bar

H Maximize

I Minimize

J Navigation pane

K Operating system

L Taskbar

M Vertical scroll bar

N Windows Aero

O Windows Explorer

Content-Based Assessments

Fill in the Blank

Write the correct word in the space provided.

1. The files and folders stored in the selected disk drive or folder are displayed in the _____ pane.

2. The working area of the Windows Vista screen—consisting of program icons, a taskbar, a Sidebar, and a Start button—is the _____.

3. A graphic representation—often a small image on a button that enables you to run a program or program function—is a(n) _____.

4. The arrow, I-beam, or other symbol that shows the location or position of the mouse on your screen is the mouse _____.

5. The _____ area is an area on the right side of the taskbar that keeps you informed about processes that are occurring in the background, such as antivirus software, network connections, and other utility programs.

6. Custom file properties such as names, places, and descriptions that are added to files are called _____.

7. You can activate a(n) _____ menu by placing the pointer over an object and clicking the right mouse button.

8. An area to the right of the Start button that contains shortcut icons for commonly used programs is the _____ _____ toolbar.

9. The button on the left side of the taskbar that is used to start programs, change system settings, find Windows help, or shut down the computer is called the _____ button.

10. An area on the right side of the screen, the Windows _____ displays useful dynamic programs, such as a clock, a stock market ticker, or a weather window.

11. A dynamic program—such as a clock, a stock market ticker, or a weather window—that display on the desktop is a(n) _____.

12. A small storage device that plugs into a computer USB port; also called a thumb drive or a USB drive, is commonly known as a(n) _____ drive.

13. The three or four characters to the right of the period in a file name, the file _____ can be hidden or displayed.

14. You can _____ a file or files to reduce the size of the files or combine files to make them easier to send.

15. When you copy an item, it is stored in the _____, a temporary storage area in Windows.

Glossary

Active window The window in which the cursor movements, commands, or text entry occur when two or more windows are open.

Address bar A toolbar that displays the organizational path to the active file, folder, or window.

Aero See Windows Aero.

All Programs Command at the bottom of the Start menu that takes you to all available programs on your computer.

Archive To back up files and store them somewhere other than the main hard drive.

Ascending order Files or folders listed from *a* to *z* when sorted.

Cascade To display the open windows on the desktop so that they line up in a diagonal line from the upper left corner of the screen downward.

CD A compact disc—an optical storage device used to store data, and which can be read-only or read-write.

Click To press the left mouse button one time.

Clipboard A temporary storage area in Windows that stores the most recently copied item.

Close button A shortcut button in a title bar that closes a window or a program.

Command bar Area at the top of a window that includes the toolbar, menu bar, address bar, and search pane.

Compress Reduce the size of a file or combine several files into one.

Computer icon An icon that represents the computer on which you are working, and that provides access to the drives, folders, and files on your computer.

Content pane Displays files and folders stored in the disk drive or folder that is currently selected in the Navigation pane.

Context-sensitive command A command associated with activities in which you are engaged; often activated by right-clicking a screen item.

Descending order Files or folders listed from *z* to *a* when sorted.

Desktop background The picture, pattern, or color that displays on the desktop.

Desktop The working area of the Windows Vista screen, consisting of program icons, a taskbar, a sidebar, and a Start button.

Details pane Displays details about the drive, folder, or file selected in the Content pane.

Dialog box A box that asks you to make a decision about an individual object or topic. Dialog boxes do not have Minimize buttons.

Dimmed An icon or menu object is gray and faded, indicating that the icon or menu object is not currently available

Double-click Press the left mouse button two times in rapid succession, using caution not to move the mouse.

Drag Move the mouse pointer while holding down the left mouse button, and then release at the appropriate time.

Drive An area of storage that is formatted with the Windows file system and that has a drive letter such as C.

DVD A digital video (or versatile) disc—an optical storage device used to store data, and which can be read-only or read-write.

Edit mode A Windows mode that enables you to change the name of a file or folder, and works the same in all Windows applications.

File Work that you save and store on a drive, such as a Word document or a PowerPoint presentation.

File extension The three or four characters to the right of the period in a file name. Extensions tell the computer the program to use to open the file. File extensions can be displayed or hidden.

Flash drive A small storage device that plugs into a computer USB port; also called a thumb drive or a USB drive.

Flip 3D A three-dimensional visual representation that enables you to flip through the windows that are open.

Folder Storage area, represented on the screen by a picture of a paper file folder, used to store files or other folders.

Folders list Part of the Navigation pane that displays the drive and folder structure on the computer.

Gadget A dynamic program—such as a clock, a stock market ticker, or a weather window—that displays on the desktop, usually in the Windows Sidebar.

Gadget controls A set of tools that include a Move button in the shape of eight small dots, an Options button in the shape of a wrench, and a Close button.

Graphical user interface (GUI) A computer interface that shows documents as they will look in their final form and uses icons to represent programs.

Guided help In the Windows Help and Support dialog box, a help technique that walks you through a process step-by-step.

Hard drive A large disk drive inside your computer, also referred to as a Local Disk.

Hardware The computer memory, disk drive space, attached devices such as printers and scanners, and the central processing unit (CPU).

Horizontal scroll bar The bar at the bottom of a window that enables you to move left and right to view information that extends beyond the left and right edges of the screen.

Icon A graphic representation; often a small image on a button that enables you to run a program or program function.

Local disk A large disk drive inside your computer, also referred to as a hard disk.

Maximize To increase the size of a window to fill the screen.

Menu A list of commands within a category.

Menu bar The bar near the top of a window that lists the names of menu categories.

Metadata Information about a file, such as tags, a title, a rating, the file name, and the file size.

Minimize To remove the window from the screen without closing it. Minimized windows can be reopened by clicking the associated button in the taskbar.

Mouse pointer The arrow, I-beam, or other symbol that shows the location or position of the mouse on your screen. Also called the pointer.

Navigation pane The pane on the left side of the Computer or Windows Explorer window that contains Personal folders and the Folders list.

Network icon An icon that represents the network to which your computer is attached, and that provides access to the drives, folders, and files on your network.

Notification area Area on the right side of the taskbar that keeps you informed about processes that are occurring in the background, such as antivirus software, network connections, and other utility programs. It also displays the time.

Operating system A set of instructions that coordinates the activities of your computer. Microsoft Windows Vista is an operating system.

Paint A program included with Vista in which graphics are created or edited.

Personal folders The top part of the Navigation pane that displays folders associated with the current user.

Pinned programs area An area at the top of the Start menu that is reserved for programs that you want to display permanently, although you can also delete programs from this area.

Pointer See mouse pointer.

Pointing Positioning the tip of the pointer in the center of an icon or other screen object.

Quick Launch toolbar An area to the right of the Start button that contains shortcut icons for commonly used programs.

Recycle Bin A storage area for files that have been deleted. Files can be recovered from the Recycle Bin or permanently removed.

Restore Return a window to the size it was before it was maximized, using the Restore Down button.

Right-click Click the right mouse button to activate a shortcut menu.

Screen saver A picture or animation that displays on your screen after a set period of computer inactivity.

ScreenTip A small box, activated by holding the pointer over a button or other screen object, that displays the name of a screen element.

Scroll box The box in the vertical and horizontal scroll bars that can be dragged to reposition the document on the screen. The size of the scroll box also indicates the relative size of the document.

Search box A box in which you type a search word or phrase.

Search folder Retains all of the search conditions you specified during your search, and re-creates the search every time you click the search folder.

Shortcut menu A menu activated by placing the pointer over an object and clicking the right mouse button.

Stacked All of the open windows display on the screen.

Start button The button on the left side of the taskbar that is used to start programs, change system settings, find Windows help, or shut down the computer.

Start menu A menu that enables you to access the programs on your computer, and also enables you to change the way Windows operates, to access and configure your network, and to get help and support when it is needed.

Status area Another name for the notification area on the right side of the taskbar.

Status bar A horizontal bar at the bottom of the document window that provides information about the current state of what you are viewing in the window, for example, the page number of a document. In some cases, the status bar also displays the name of the window.

Submenu A second-level menu activated by selecting a menu option.

System tray Another name for the notification area on the right side of the taskbar.

Tags Custom file properties such as names, places, and descriptions that are added to files to enable you to categorize and find files more quickly.

Taskbar Displays the Start button and the name of any open documents. The taskbar may also display shortcut buttons for other programs.

Thumb drive A small storage device that plugs into a computer USB port; also called a USB drive or a flash drive.

Thumbnail A miniature representation of the contents of a window or file.

Title bar Displays the program icon, the name of the document, and the name of the program. The Minimize, Maximize/Restore Down, and Close buttons are grouped on the right side of the title bar.

Toolbar A row of buttons that activate commands, such as Undo or Bold, with a single click of the left mouse button.

USB drive A small storage device that plugs into a computer USB port; also called a thumb drive or a flash drive.

Vertical scroll bar The bar at the right side of a window that enables you to move up and down to view information that extends beyond the top and bottom of the screen.

Welcome Center By default, a window that displays every time you start your computer, and displays links to a number of topics, including upgrading Windows, connecting to the Internet, adding new users, and taking advantage of special offers from Microsoft.

Wildcard A character, such as an asterisk, that can be used to match any number of characters in a file search.

Window A box that displays information or a program, such as a letter, Excel, or a calculator. Windows usually consist of title bars, toolbars, menu bars, and status bars. A window will always have a Minimize button.

Window name The name of the window or program, displayed in the status bar or title bar.

Windows An operating system that coordinates the activities of a computer.

Windows Aero The Vista user interface that features a three-dimensional look, with transparent window frames, live previews of open windows, and multiple color schemes. Aero is an acronym for **A**uthentic, **E**nergetic, **R**eflective, **O**pen.

Windows Explorer A program that enables you to create and manage folders, and manage copy, move, sort, and delete files.

Windows Sidebar An area on the right side of the screen that displays useful Gadgets, such as a clock, a stock market ticker, or a weather map.

WordPad A simple word processing program that comes with Windows Vista.

Index

SINGLE PC LICENSE AGREEMENT AND LIMITED WARRANTY

READ THIS LICENSE CAREFULLY BEFORE OPENING THIS PACKAGE. BY OPENING THIS PACKAGE, YOU ARE AGREEING TO THE TERMS AND CONDITIONS OF THIS LICENSE. IF YOU DO NOT AGREE, DO NOT OPEN THE PACKAGE. PROMPTLY RETURN THE UNOPENED PACKAGE AND ALL ACCOMPANYING ITEMS TO THE PLACE YOU OBTAINED THEM. *THESE TERMS APPLY TO ALL LICENSED SOFTWARE ON THE DISK EXCEPT THAT THE TERMS FOR USE OF ANY SHAREWARE OR FREEWARE ON TH E DISKETTES ARE AS SET FORTH IN THE ELECTRONIC LICENSE LOCATED ON THE DISK:*

1. GRANT OF LICENSE and OWNERSHIP: The enclosed computer programs ("Software") are licensed, not sold, to you by Prentice-Hall, Inc. ("We" or the "Company") and in consideration of your purchase or adoption of the accompanying Company textbooks and/or other materials, and your agreement to these terms. We reserve any rights not granted to you. You own only the disk(s) but we and/or our licensors own the Software itself. This license allows you to use and display your copy of the Software on a single computer (i.e., with a single CPU) at a single location for academic use only, so long as you comply with the terms of this Agreement. You may make one copy for back up, or transfer your copy to another CPU, provided that the Software is usable on only one computer.

2. RESTRICTIONS: You may not transfer or distribute the Software or documentation to anyone else. Except for backup, you may not copy the documentation or the Software. You may not network the Software or otherwise use it on more than one computer or computer terminal at the same time. You may not reverse engineer, disassemble, decompile, modify, adapt, translate, or create derivative works based on the Software or the Documentation. You may be held legally responsible for any copying or copyright infringement which is caused by your failure to abide by the terms of these restrictions.

3. TERMINATION: This license is effective until terminated. This license will terminate automatically without notice from the Company if you fail to comply with any provisions or limitations of this license. Upon termination, you shall destroy the Documentation and all copies of the Software. All provisions of this Agreement as to limitation and disclaimer of warranties, limitation of liability, remedies or damages, and our ownership rights shall survive termination.

4. DISCLAIMER OF WARRANTY: THE COMPANY AND ITS LICENSORS MAKE NO WARRANTIES ABOUT THE SOFTWARE, WHICH IS PROVIDED "AS-IS." IF THE DISK IS DEFECTIVE IN MATERIALS OR WORKMANSHIP, YOUR ONLY REMEDY IS TO RETURN IT TO THE COMPANY WITHIN 30 DAYS FOR REPLACEMENT UNLESS THE COMPANY DETERMINES IN GOOD FAITH THAT THE DISK HAS BEEN MISUSED OR IMPROPERLY INSTALLED, REPAIRED, ALTERED OR DAMAGED. THE COMPANY DISCLAIMS ALL WARRANTIES, EXPRESS OR IMPLIED, INCLUDING WITHOUT LIMITATION, THE IMPLIED WARRANTIES OF MERCHANTABILITY AND FITNESS FOR A PARTICULAR PURPOSE. THE COMPANY DOES NOT WARRANT, GUARANTEE OR MAKE ANY REPRESENTATION REGARDING THE ACCURACY, RELIABILITY, CURRENTNESS, USE, OR RESULTS OF USE, OF THE SOFTWARE.

5. LIMITATION OF REMEDIES AND DAMAGES: IN NO EVENT, SHALL THE COMPANY OR ITS EMPLOYEES, AGENTS, LICENSORS OR CONTRACTORS BE LIABLE FOR ANY INCIDENTAL, INDIRECT, SPECIAL OR CONSEQUENTIAL DAMAGES ARISING OUT OF OR IN CONNECTION WITH THIS LICENSE OR THE SOFTWARE, INCLUDING, WITHOUT LIMITATION, LOSS OF USE, LOSS OF DATA, LOSS OF INCOME OR PROFIT, OR OTHER LOSSES SUSTAINED AS A RESULT OF INJURY TO ANY PERSON, OR LOSS OF OR DAMAGE TO PROPERTY, OR CLAIMS OF THIRD PARTIES, EVEN IF THE COMPANY OR AN AUTHORIZED REPRESENTATIVE OF THE COMPANY HAS BEEN ADVISED OF THE POSSIBILITY OF SUCH DAMAGES. SOME JURISDICTIONS DO NOT ALLOW THE LIMITATION OF DAMAGES IN CERTAIN CIRCUMSTANCES, SO THE ABOVE LIMITATIONS MAY NOT ALWAYS APPLY.

6. GENERAL: THIS AGREEMENT SHALL BE CONSTRUED IN ACCORDANCE WITH THE LAWS OF THE UNITED STATES OF AMERICA AND THE STATE OF NEW YORK, APPLICABLE TO CONTRACTS MADE IN NEW YORK, AND SHALL BENEFIT THE COMPANY, ITS AFFILIATES AND ASSIGNEES. This Agreement is the complete and exclusive statement of the agreement between you and the Company and supersedes all proposals, prior agreements, oral or written, and any other communications between you and the company or any of its representatives relating to the subject matter. If you are a U.S. Government user, this Software is licensed with "restricted rights" as set forth in subparagraphs (a)-(d) of the Commercial Computer-Restricted Rights clause at FAR 52.227-19 or in subparagraphs (c)(1)(ii) of the Rights in Technical Data and Computer Software clause at DFARS 252.227-7013, and similar clauses, as applicable.

Should you have any questions concerning this agreement or if you wish to contact the Company for any reason, please contact in writing:

Multimedia Production
Higher Education Division
Prentice-Hall, Inc.
1 Lake Street
Upper Saddle River NJ 07458